Morning Momentum

Tactics You Never Thought of

For Launching an Unstoppable Day

2

Morning Momentum

Tactics You Never Thought of

For Launching an Unstoppable Day

Rick Grubbs

Supplemental material for each chapter is available at
MorningMomentumBook.com.

More resources for Biblical time management are available at
LifeChangingSeminars.com.

Your comments to the author are welcome at:

LifeChanging Seminars

285 Majestic Dr.

Salisbury NC 28146

Rick@LifeChangingSeminars.com

CONTENTS

-Three simple steps to planning your time each day
-A cure for the frustration of "not getting it all done"

5. Morning Devotions47

Big Rocks First (Matthew 6:33)

-Tactics for staying awake during morning devotions
-Avoiding weapons of mass distraction
-The first thing George Mueller did each day (It's not what you think!)

6. The Morning Commute55

How to Make it Count

-The "minimize and maximize" strategy
-Redeeming the time in the car – Use your ears, mouth and mind
-When public transit is an option
-Contrarian tactics and alternatives to the daily commute

7. Starting the Workday69

Setting the Tempo / Staying in Control

-Avoid morning temptations and interruptions that will sidetrack your entire day
-Be a guest, not a host
-Do the "Worst First"
-The best time to have your coffee
-Starting your workday with energy, enthusiasm, and vision

8. A Successful Morning Starts the Night Before......76

Get your Stuff and Your Self Ready for Bed on Time

-The Biblical day actually begins with the evening before
-Do's and don'ts for the last hour
-Use John Wesley's method of determining your bedtime

"He that walks with wise men shall be wise." Pr. 13.20
-Biblical examples of early rising
-Great Christians who practiced early rising
-Correlations between early rising and financial success, with contemporary examples
-Learning from negative examples

Adapting Principles to Different Circumstances

-Night Owls *or "What if I'm just not a morning person?"*
-Students
-Parents of newborns
-Home Educators
-Working from home
-Retired
-Sick and tired
-Traveling, Vacations and Weekends

Making it a Lifelong Habit

-What you need to know about habit formation
-What to do when you fail
-Seeing the bigger picture-The rewards of delayed gratification
-Procrastination is the assassination of your motivation- Begin NOW!

Chapter 1

Why Mornings Matter

"I don't know all the keys to success, but one of the keys to failure is to continually start your day out wrong."

A successful *life* is simply an accumulation of successful *days*. Experience enough successful days, and you will have experienced a successful life. It's that simple.

The question is, *"How do you have a successful day?"* That answer is found in an old proverb that says, *"As goes the morning, so goes the day."*

God gives you 24 hours every day, the most important being the very first. That's because it sets the tone for the following 23. Life begins anew every morning. Patterns of diligence or laziness, pleasantness or grumpiness, and following God's plan versus my own agenda, are commonly established during the first hour of the day.

Starting well doesn't mean you will *always* finish well. But starting well enables you to finish well. When my four year old buttons his shirt, the main thing he has to do is get the first button lined up right. The rest is easy. But if the first button is out of alignment it will be impossible to finish the job correctly.

Your daily success requires the same strategy. You cannot concentrate and focus your efforts on the entire day. That would not be focusing at all. Center your attention on the part of the day with the greatest payoff. That is mornings.

Concentrate on creating a strong momentum in the morning, and you will establish an industrious mindset early on that will benefit you the rest of the day. Popping up on the right side of the bed sets in motion an upbeat mood and tempo for the day. It's the first step to charting a day you will finish with no regrets.

Morning Characters Have Character

We know mornings matter because a clear majority of accomplished individuals are "morning people." In chapter 9, we will meet inspiring examples of high achievers past and present, Christian and nonbeliever, whose exceptional lives daily begin with morning momentum. People of great achievement may not be 100% early birds, but it's pretty close. That's because there is a direct cause and effect between mastering mornings and a life of accomplishment.

Lasting accomplishment is the natural outcome of good character. The Bible calls it "The fruit of the Spirit." The opportune time to develop good character qualities is in the morning. Character is largely formed through the decisions we make when no one is looking. Opportunities to strengthen your character arise with morning choices such as whether to hit the snooze when you know you shouldn't or cut devotions short to focus on something "more urgent." A consistent, well planned morning routine accelerates your character formation. Since your character determines your destiny, mastering your mornings is the fast track to changing your destiny.

Opportunity Knocks in the Morning

Mornings matter because each one brings a fresh window of opportunity available only to those who are sharp enough to take advantage of it. One of the distinguishing traits of those who rise to the top is the habit of making time for their *opportunities*, not just their obligations. Mornings offer a unique set of circumstances for the few who are sufficiently motivated to seize opportunity.

An hour in the morning nearly always has greater potential for cultivating opportunity than an hour at any other time of day. In the quiet of the morning your mind is fresh and clear, ready to be tapped for important problem solving and creative thinking. There are fewer interruptions in the morning. No ringing phones or drop in visitors means we stay focused longer on those high payoff projects that require a deeper concentration which we can't generate any other time of day.

Early birds catch more than worms. Mornings have gold in them for those who rise up early enough to do the mining. While most of the world is sleeping away their opportunities, morning people are already stoked and starting to produce.

Get Control of Yourself

Mornings matter because morning people are the most proactive. They understand delayed gratification. They have chosen to go against their natural inclinations by denying themselves a short term pleasure to obtain a far better reward in the future.[1] That is the essence of Biblical thinking.

Being proactive means staying ahead of the crowd. Rising up before the sun is not easy. But it gives you a jump on the day that energizes body and mind. Stress levels decrease when you are controlling your time instead of time controlling you.

Mornings Matter Because Time Matters

On May 30, 2015, Harriet Thompson completed the San Diego Marathon in 7 hours and 24 minutes. That might not sound very significant, except for the fact that Harriet was born in 1923, and at 92 years old she became the oldest woman ever to finish a marathon.

Harriet Thompson didn't run her first race until she was in her 70's. But you and I are in a race today. It is a race with time. The goal of this race is to see how much we can do for God between now and the day we die. Winning that race requires springing into action the moment the starter pistol sounds. It requires morning momentum.

There is a popular quote, of unknown origin, that expresses this idea well:

Every morning in Africa, a gazelle wakes up. It knows it must run faster than the fastest lion or it will be eaten. Every morning a lion also wakes up. It knows it must outrun the slowest gazelle or it will starve to death. So, it doesn't matter whether you are a lion or a gazelle: when the sun comes up, you'd better be running.

Time is our most valuable earthly possession. Queen Elizabeth I of England was the richest person in the world. Yet as she lay on her deathbed, her last words were, "I would give all my kingdom for one more moment of time." Ben Franklin asked the question, "Do you love life? Then don't waste your time, for that is what life is made of." He's also the one who made the most well know case for morning momentum when he said:

Early to bed,
Early to rise,
Makes a man healthy, wealthy, and wise.

Ben was right. An early start is a good start. But there is one more reason why mornings matter. And it is even more important than becoming healthy, wealthy, or wise.

Mornings Matter to God

This isn't simply a book about how to become "successful" as man views success. I want you to experience success that lasts forever, not just the brief 70 or so years we live in this world. Success that doesn't aspire beyond that is so temporary that it loses all significance when viewed in retrospect 10,000 years from today.

You are a three part being: Physical, mental and spiritual. That's why our focus will be on creating morning momentum physically, mentally and most important, spiritually.

Certainly God can and does meet with people at all hours of the day. But it is clear from scripture that God especially loves to meet with people in the morning. Scripture is filled with examples of those who rose early for a special meeting with God.[2]

While mornings might not seem like a heavenly experience to some of us, God even uses morning as a picture of Heaven. [3] Times of spiritual renewal are referred to both in Scripture and in Church history as "awakenings."[4] Also, one of the titles given to The Lord Himself is the "Morning Star."[5]

If we want to live a life pleasing to God and to be open to His blessing, we have to learn to think God's thoughts, which are usually opposite of our thoughts.[6] By nature we are not generally inclined to rise early to invest time getting God's perspective and instructions for the day. But for those who do, the payoff is tremendous. Imagine the regret the women at the empty tomb would have faced had they slept in and missed being part of the greatest event in history. We are told that Jesus' resurrection occurred, "very early in the morning."[7]

Creating morning momentum is all about obeying God from the very first moment of your day. Reaching your full potential of all God has planned for you each day requires yielding to Him without hesitation. While we recognize and agree with that truth in theory, we also know how easy it is to dismiss that fact in a warm bed on a cold morning.

"Good" Morning?

"Good morning" is a friendly greeting in most any language. Yet for many of us, "good morning" is an oxymoron, a contradiction of terms. Mornings are anything but good. They are often the most stressful time of the day.[8]

That stress comes from a lack of control over our mornings. The person who gets up late and unprepared just lost control. They now have fewer options for the day. A life with fewer options is a life of bondage and slavery. By contrast, getting up early creates more options for the day and a greater sense of freedom.

It is no exaggeration to say that learning morning momentum is the quickest way to initiate success in every area of life. Improving your health, career, finances, relationships, or spiritual life, requires finding focused, uninterrupted time to strategize and create growth in each area. By following the methods I'm about to explain, you can see real change before 8:00 tomorrow morning.

Are you excited yet about doing mornings differently? In the next chapter, we'll get practical by learning some tactics for creating a good morning. It all starts with getting the first minute right.

Chapter 2

Your First Minute

How to Soar Out of Bed like a Human Cannonball!

Lasers are powerful. They take energy that would otherwise be broadly scattered, and focus it on one very precise spot. Let's now generates some power by focusing not just on the first hour, but "laser focusing" on the most important minute within that hour.

God gives you 1440 minutes each day. Get the first one right and you'll set in motion a domino effect of success for the following 1439. If time is money, investing in a successful first minute yields exponential returns. It's leveraging on steroids!

There are three things you must do in your first minute:

1. Wake Up
2. Get Up
3. Stay Up

For most of us, that sequence starts with the electronic rooster we call an "alarm clock." There's our first problem.

Don't Be Alarmed

An "alarm" signals something terrible is about to happen! Your smoke alarm means your house is about to burn down. Your burglar alarm means someone is threatening your family's safety. An air-raid alarm means take cover or be killed!

I like motivational expert Zig Ziglar's idea of renaming the wake-up device an "opportunity clock." There's no reason to get "alarmed" first thing every morning when you can view each new day as an opportunity instead! Someone said getting old can be depressing until you consider the alternative. The same is true with getting up.

Every day you wake up is a new opportunity which some folks weren't blessed with that morning. View it that way and you'll realize there would be cause for alarm if we *didn't* wake up. But since we did, there's opportunity! The writer of Lamentations puts it this way *"It is of the Lord's mercies that we are not consumed, because his compassions fail not. They are new every morning."*[9]

Now that we know what to call it, let's determine the best method for using the opportunity clock.

Snoozers are Losers

Most opportunity clocks come with a self-defeating design flaw. Most people call it a "snooze" button. I call it a "lose" button, because if you choose to snooze you choose to lose!

I fought my own battle with the snooze several years ago. When my clock sounded, I would roll over, smack it, and fall back in bed. Ten minutes later the process would repeat itself, as I counted through the "Boeing numbers."

Just like the Boeing aircraft, I started out at 7:27. Ten minutes later a 7:37 would come through. Then a 7:47, or even a 7:57! Finally, about 8:00, I would jump out of bed and rush out the door, without spending time with God. This became my daily pattern until I discovered this verse in Proverbs:

As the door turns on its hinges,
so does the lazy man on his bed.[10]

I thought, "That's a picture of me: A lover of the covers in a wrestling match with my sheets and getting pinned!" So I cut the wires to the snooze. Now when the clock sounded, I knew I had been served my one and only notice. I had to get up, so I did.

I also moved the clock to the other side of the room. That meant I had to escape the bed's grasp by marching across the room and shutting it off. By the time I did all that, I was "up," and "up" is where I already determined I should now be if I was to spend time with the Lord.

As one comedian pointed out, "If you really think about it, hitting the snooze button in the morning doesn't even make sense. It's like saying, 'I hate getting up in the morning—so I do it over... and over... and over again.'[11]

Your first assignment then is getting the right clock in the right place. It may require some searching to find a snooze-free clock. If you can't find one right away, at least tape a giant "NO!" sign over the snooze button or glue a loaded mousetrap on it.

"There's an App for That"

You probably already have a "no snooze" opportunity clock on your phone or tablet. Check your settings for an option to turn off the snooze. There are also a growing number of innovative apps for the waking challenged. Some post your wake up time on Facebook, while others monitor your circadian rhythms or require you to shake them before they will turn off. Just remember, if you use your phone for a wake up device, avoid the temptation to keep it beside the bed.

The last thing I do each night is read the Bible in bed on my phone -- something I recommend. But if you do so, make sure to use your last gasp of energy before falling asleep to toss the phone out of reach, maybe on a pillow or thick carpet. Remember, every minute you snooze is likely a minute spent outside the will of God. You can't afford that, especially first thing in the morning when you are setting a precedent for the day.

Other Clock Tactics

Custom Message Clocks. I remember as a child in the 1960's looking forward to getting up early on Christmas. I was so intent on it that I used the latest technology to make sure I got up as early as I could. I plugged a cassette tape player into a timer which was set to play a recording of me telling myself to wake up and get my new toys. It never failed to work!

Phones, tablets, and other devices can record custom messages and play them at a set time. Just record whatever message, positive or negative, you need to get yourself up. You can remind yourself of a special event that day, quote some Scripture, or even preach yourself a hard sermon on the consequences of oversleeping.

Like a child on Christmas morning, if the motivation is there, you will get up. You just have to find creative ways to make every day "Christmas".

Waking to Music. There are two strategies here: Music you like and music you don't like.

The first option is a good Christian radio station or a playlist that especially appeals to you as a wakeup call to worship. But the opposite approach can work as well.

I once stayed overnight with a friend who has a very close walk with God. I was surprised the next morning when his clock radio blared out some very ungodly music. He explained he set it to that station because he couldn't stand to listen to it so he would jump out of bed immediately to silence it. If he listened to music he enjoyed, he would fall back asleep.

Natural Alarm Clock. If you want a natural and effective strategy that doesn't cost anything and is guaranteed to work, drink a large glass of water just before going to bed. When you wake up, you will definitely have to get up!

If you have not yet discovered the online resources for every chapter of this book, now is a great time. I've highlighted there some very unique clocks such as the train horn, the bed shaker, and clocks that make you chase them around the room to shut them off. Visit MorningMomentumBook.com for some novel ideas. There was one idea that was so over-the-top I had to mention it here as well.

Money Shredder. This has to be the world's most ruthless wake up device. I read of one fellow who connected a paper shredder and an opportunity clock to a timer so they both came on at the same time. He then taped a $20 bill to the bottom of a sheet of paper and inserted it into the shredder. That meant when the clock (and shredder) kicked on, he had only seconds to rescue his $20 from being shredded. I've never tried this myself, but I can't imagine anyone for whom it would *not* work!

Of course, for $20 you could just pay a neighbor to come drag you out of bed each day, which brings me to our next tactic: Accountability!

Ask for Help!

Biblical archeologists recently discovered the reason it took 40 years for the Israelites to cross over into the Promised Land: They had all male leadership so nobody wanted to ask directions. That joke reveals something about us men. We just don't like asking for help.

But when it comes to getting up on time, we all do better when we know someone is keeping us accountable. Effective managers understand that people don't do what you *expect,* they do what you *inspect.* If you want to shoot out of bed like a human cannonball, it helps to have someone appointed to light your fuse each day.

I once attended a large church with a 5:00 AM prayer meeting seven days a week. I asked the pastor if I could be responsible for unlocking the church for the meeting. Since it wasn't exactly a crowded event, he was delighted to find someone who wanted that job! The next day, when my clock went off, I immediately got up, because I knew if I didn't, someone would know about it. They would not be able to get into the church for prayer because Rick Grubbs was lazy that morning. That commitment got me up on time more consistently than anything I've ever tried.

When my wife and I were missionaries in Eastern Europe, we had no local supervision and no assigned schedule. My wake up discipline soon evaporated. The solution for me was to voluntarily send the mission director a monthly report detailing what time I got up each day. The desire to preserve my good reputation outweighed my desire to soak a few more minutes in a warm bed on a cold day.

Post your waking time for the whole world to see on a blog, Facebook, or refrigerator calendar. Give others permission to ask about it. Maybe they never will, but just knowing the possibility exists might give you an added weight to tip the scales in favor of "mind over mattress."

On another occasion, I found a like-minded friend who also needed some accountability. We lived a block apart. We would meet half way each morning, unless the other person didn't show. In that case we were to go to their house and bang on the door until they answered. Since our wives and babies didn't necessarily wish to get up at that hour, we both had a powerful incentive to do the right

22

thing, first thing each day! We did allow an excused absence so long as we posted it on the front door the night before.[12]

Meeting someone outside your home is probably the best form of accountability, because you have to be fully awake and physically active to do it. But when that's impractical you can still make a phone appointment and largely accomplish the same thing. Give your partner permission to keep calling until you respond.

Of course, your accountability partner can be someone from your own home. The advantage here is you can give them permission to jerk the sheets off and yank your unresponsive body out of bed. That's a great way to apply the following verses from Ecclesiastes (my application notes included):

Two are better than one because they have a good return for their labor. For if either of them falls [back asleep], the one will lift up his companion. But woe to the one who falls when there is not another to lift him up [from the bed!].
Ecclesiastes 4: 9, 10

God made us to need one another, so there is likely someone who needs your help as much as you need theirs. Morning accountability is great for encouraging one another to do the right thing.[13]

There are two occasions when you can get up: When you really have to and when you really want to. Alarms and accountability create "*have to*." Now let's generate some "*want to*."

Leverage the Power of God's Word

The most powerful weapon for initiating any change of habit is the Word of God. So look for creative methods to use that Word as a lever to pry you from the bed.[14]

One tactic is to mount scripture on the ceiling over your bed warning you of the dangers of laziness. Imagine the impact of opening your eyes first thing each morning and seeing a verse like this one:

A little sleep, a little slumber, a little folding of the hands to rest: So shall your poverty come as a prowler and your need like an armed man.
Proverbs 24: 33, 34

Use your phone to record select verses on your in your own voice with compelling reasons to break the bondage of lethargic sleep and laziness. Here are some suggestions:

- *How long will you lie there, you sluggard? When will you get up from your sleep? Proverbs 6:9*

- *Go to the ant, you sluggard; consider her ways, and be wise. Proverbs 6:6*

- *A sluggard does not plow in season; so at harvest time he looks but finds nothing. Proverbs 20:4*

The greatest spiritual warfare of your day often takes place during the first minute. So be prepared. Let these, and other verses like them, paint a graphic picture in your mind of missed opportunities which God specially prepared for you in the day ahead. Picture the cumulative result of a life wasted through procrastination which began each morning as you slept through God's appointed start time.

Consider the disappointment you will be to God, to yourself, and to others who depend on you, if you ignore God's prompting during the first decision of the day by failing to seize the moment. Contrast that with the sense of accomplishment that comes with slaying the dragons unleashed by your spiritual foe and launching your day in a note of victory before you even reach the shower!

What Time Should I Get Up?

First, remember that even minor adjustments in time can make a big difference, like the marriage counselor who told his client to give his wife a compliment. "Tell her she looks like the first day of spring," he instructed. The absent-minded husband, however, missed it by a day when he told her, "You look like the last day of a long, cold winter."

Likewise, a small adjustment in rising time could make a big difference. Instead of setting your clock for 6:00, turn it back one minute to 5:59. Now you can tell your friends, "I get up at 5 something every morning." The extra minute gives you bragging rights and promotes you to a whole different epic class of superhero early risers.

In our seminars I ask, "How many of you would like an extra two week vacation next year?" Usually about 95% raise their hands. Then I ask, "If you really wanted to, or if you really had to, how many of you could get up just 15 minutes earlier than you've been getting up?" About 90% will again raise their hands. Then I show how rising just 15 minutes earlier each day adds 92 hours each year to your life. That's more than two 40 hour work weeks of vacation!

Take it a step further by going to an extreme, at least occasionally. If you normally get up at 7:00 and you move it back to 6:45 that might not make enough impact. But if you set your clock for 3:30, the sheer shock of waking up at that hour will give you an adrenalin jolt! You can't do it every day, but when you need some extended time with God or special momentum for an important project, being an "extremist" is an option.

Staying Up

In your first minute not only must you wake up and get up, but you have to stay up. You do that by burning your bridges. Make your decision to get up irreversible both physically and mentally. Jesus commends those who make a right decision and refuse to reconsider it.[15] Scripture also warns that, *"A double minded man is unstable in all his ways."*[16]

The first question you face each day is not, "Should I get up now?" That question was determined and settled the night before. The first question you must answer is "Will I obey God right now?" Don't hesitate, cogitate, marinate, prognosticate or debate. Just initiate and participate!

Once you have broken contact with the bed, get some bright light shining. Light dispels darkness and messages your body to get moving. If you plan to get up after sunrise, open your blinds before you go to bed at night so the room will be flooded with bright, natural sunlight when you wake up. Solomon wrote, "Truly the light is sweet, and it is pleasant for the eyes to behold the sun."[17] Don't be like the fellow who said, "If God wanted me to see the sunrise He would have scheduled it later in the day." Move your bed into the light as needed or buy an appliance timer to turn the lights on for you at wake up time.

A few days ago our family passed a bar on our evening walk. My seven year old commented on how bars are always dark places. Then we talked about how spiritual and physical darkness often go together. Turning on the light first thing in the morning changes the atmosphere from night to day and changes the mood from drowsiness to alertness.

Once the light is on, make your bed (assuming your spouse is not still sleeping!). Maybe you heard about the guy who married a perfectionist. He got up in the middle of the night to go to the bathroom and returned to discover his wife had already made the bed!

Don't take it that far, but do apply the Scripture, *"make not provision for the flesh."*[18] An unmade bed is a giant electromagnet pulling your body back into a horizontal position. You disable it by covering it ASAP before it snares you. Don't worry about getting it military perfect. No one is going to inspect it. Just get it done quickly.

Verbal Momentum

The final step in waking up is to use a quickly spoken word to create momentum. Make a quick prayer to God simply expressing thanks for another day and telling Him, "Good morning." This is not your morning devotions. That comes later after you are thoroughly awake. This is just a quick acknowledgement of the Lord to dispel the darkness and get you in sync with God from your waking moment. You can do it as you are leaving the bed, walking across the room to shut off the opportunity clock, or while making the bed.

You can also give a short, one or two line motivational speech to yourself as you rise, such as:

- "This is the day the Lord has made. I will rejoice and be glad in it!"
- "What a great day to get up and go get 'em."
- Pretend you are Superman. Extend a fist and shout, "Up, Up and Away!" as you leave the bed.

Having some fun with it will change the first minute from something you dread to something you actually anticipate!

Points to Remember:

- Three things to do during your first minute: Wake up, Get up, and Stay up!

- Five extra minutes of sleep between snooze alarms is not going to prevent you from being tired that day.

- When you wake up, get up. And when you get up, wake up!

- If you believe God has power to raise you from the dead, don't you believe He has power to raise you from the bed?

- Change how you wake up and you will change your entire life.

Chapter 3

Streamlining Your Morning Routine

At the end of World War II, US efficiency experts helped rebuild the war torn Japanese auto factories. They made a science of "lean manufacturing" with a constant focus on refining content, sequence, and timing to improve efficiency. Each of the small gains produced by meticulously refining prescribed movements was multiplied by repetition, and by the 1970's Toyota had replaced Detroit as the world's #1 auto maker.

Could there be more effective methods to get your day underway than what you are now using? If so, what would your ideal morning look like? In this chapter, I'll offer some ideas you may not have considered for gaining morning momentum by tweaking your morning routine. Over time the results can be significant.

Start with a Power Shower

Once you've broken free of the bed, advance your forward charge by reaching the shower ASAP. That's where your new high efficiency routine begins- with two towels.

Most people climb out of the shower and dry off with a single towel. The problem with that is, the towel generally reaches a point of saturation where it loses some of its effectiveness before you get completely dry. That leaves you trying to finish the job using a wet towel. By getting two towels ready, you can use one for heavy drying and another for finishing the job.[19]

This little technique may seem trivial. But if it saves you just 30 seconds per day, over the next 14 years you could spend 40 less hours drying off! That's a full work week. Wouldn't you like it if your boss gave you an extra week off for family time, volunteering at church, or just doing something you enjoy more than drying off?

Everyone has a brilliant idea in the shower. But those ideas are harder to hold onto than a bar of wet soap. They slip away before we can latch onto them. Prepping for a power shower means having a system in place, such as a note pad or the voice recorder on your phone, to capture those ideas before they evaporate with the shower mist.

Those ideas come more frequently when we actively seek them. God will speak our daily instructions when we are ready to listen and He often starts speaking in the shower. The Proverbs tell how to get direction from God: "In all your ways acknowledge Him and He shall direct your paths.[20]" We can acknowledge God in the shower by praying out loud, quoting Scripture, or singing to the Lord as we shower.[21] Spiritual multitasking pays off in the shower as we point our gaze toward the Father first thing every morning.

Form Routines not Ruts

As you develop new morning habits, such as power showers, it's important to develop routines, but not ruts. There is a huge difference:

Streamlined Morning Routine	Morning Rut
A set of life-enhancing, efficient methods of doing God's will.	A rut is a grave with both ends knocked out.
Creative approaches to daily tasks, developed over time, by listening to the promptings of God's Spirit in the morning hours	The default result of unthinking human drudgery.
Does common things in an uncommon way.	Does what comes naturally. Displays no initiative.

Constantly striving to improve. Focuses on creating a day of greater usefulness to God and others.	Self-centered. Lazy. Content with the way things are.
Produces freedom	Results in bondage
Creates momentum for the day	Kills momentum. Launches a pattern of plodding through the day

Your morning routine is a collection of habits. Those habits will either be momentum killers (ruts) or momentum builders. Four key opportunities for creating momentum builders are: Exercise, Dressing for Success, Good Attitude Formation and Breakfast.

Exercise

Your first task each morning is to get thoroughly awake. The alternative to showering yourself awake first thing is exercising yourself awake before the shower. There are multiple advantages to morning exercise over any other time of day. In his book, *8 Minutes in the Morning*, Jorge Cruise lists several of them:[22]

- Morning is the time of day most people can control. There is less opportunity for distraction and rationalization. As the day progresses, we find more excuses for not exercising. We end up procrastinating till bedtime.

- Morning exercisers stay with it three times better. A 500 person study from Mollen Clinic in Phoenix showed only 25% of evening exercisers consistently did their routines. 75% of morning exercisers stuck to it.

- Morning exercise boosts metabolism. When you first wake up, your metabolism is sluggish from sleeping. When you exercise, it increases. Thus you increase metabolism when it is naturally slowest. The advantage is that you get the maximum metabolic benefit by burning more calories at a time when you would normally be burning the least.

- Metabolism naturally spikes sometime after midday. But by exercising early in the morning, you increase your metabolism immediately so you can reap the benefits all day long.

One word of caution. I've learned from experience that if you are sleepy and hit the floor to do sit-ups or push-ups you may not get up for another hour! Till you get in practice, it's better to take a brisk walk or exercise in a stand up position, such as jumping jacks. If you can't exercise, at least have a good stretch.

Dress for Success Before You Regress

Even if you don't shower or exercise, it is vital to shed the pajamas ASAP. Doing so sends a message to your balking body that the day has begun. It is irreversible and we are now moving forward, like it or not.

Getting dressed can actually be fun if you make a game of it. Challenge yourself to see how fast you can go from PJ's to pinstripes. For example, I hate tying ties, so I leave them hanging in the closet pre-tied. I slip them over my head and tighten them in a matter of seconds.

There are practical reasons for learning to dress quickly. Once you have your shoes on they act as a counterweight to keep you from falling back in bed. And you'll not want to get a shirt wrinkled and have to iron it again after sleeping in it. Getting dressed makes an investment in the new day. You now have skin in the game and it would cost too much to turn back.

Maybe you've heard the expression, "He puts his pants on one leg at a time." It means "He's just an ordinary person." Because everyone puts their pants on one leg at a time. Everyone, that is, except firemen.

Firemen jump into their clothes with both feet at the same time because they realize that when someone is trapped in a burning building, how quickly they can get dressed and out the door is a matter of life or death. They streamline their exit procedures because of their extreme sense of urgency.

As Christians, we too have an urgent task. We live in a world that is also in big trouble and they need our help. We know it intellectually, but most of us have trouble implementing that knowledge into boots on the ground morning momentum.

Waking Up Grumpy

A bumper sticker read, "Most mornings I wake up grumpy...But some days I just let him sleep."

If you have a spouse or kids, you may be charged with "waking up Grumpy." One of the great mysteries of the universe is how kids can protest and resist sleep so vehemently at bedtime and just a few hours later love the same bed so much they cannot part with it.

Scripture teaches us to not be overcome with evil, but to overcome evil with good.[23] Having a sense of humor and expressing the joy of the Lord, whether we feel like it or not, is one way to apply that principle to the morning routine.[24] Here are some possibilities for lightening up the wake up drill while still getting the job done:

- Full volume march music! How could you sleep through Reveille or a rousing John Phillip Souza rendition of Stars and Stripes Forever?

- Sing the "Good Morning to You" song. Here's the lyrics if it's been a while since first grade for you:

  Good Morning, good morning to you.
  We're all in our places
  With sunshiny faces,
  And this is the way
  To start a new day!

  Good morning to you
  Good morning to you
  Our day is beginning
  There's so much to do.
  So good morning, good morning, good morning to you

- Be quick to praise any movement in the right direction. When asked what he hoped the final words at his funeral would be, an optimist replied, "Wait! Look, he's moving!"

- Make a fun contest of seeing who can be first to get dressed. Resort to bribery, if need be, by giving a prize for the first one to the breakfast table.

- Physically lift them out of the bed and stand them up on their feet. (OK, they may not always think this one is funny, especially after they are teens)

Getting up on the right side of the bed not only sets the mood for your own day, but for all those in your household. God calls all of us to be encouragers who "provoke one another to love and good works."[25] Lots of us are good at "provoking" family members or roommates in the morning. We just need to remember the last part of that verse.

Here's a final thought on waking up Grumpy. Developing Godly, self-disciplined character is the most important objective of child training.

As long as you keep volunteering to take responsibility for getting them out of bed they will let you do it. The parent's goal is to transfer that responsibility to the children at the earliest age possible. Training our children to get themselves up on time is part of developing a healthy work ethic, which is foundational to future success.

"Sitting Up and Taking Nourishment"

Nutrition is the source of energy behind anything you accomplish during your day. It is outside of my expertise to advise you on the best food combinations to maximize your energy, but there are gazillions of people who will. Find a few who aren't trying to sell you something and experiment with their advice till you find what works for you.

In an article, *"5 Things Super Successful People do Before 8 AM"*, Forbes.com lists # 3 as "Eat a healthy breakfast." They say:

We all know that rush out the door with a cup of coffee and an empty stomach feeling. You sit down at your desk, and you're already wondering how early that taco truck sets up camp outside your office. No good. Take that extra time in the morning to fuel your body for the tasks ahead of it. It will help keep your mind on what's at hand and not your growling stomach. Not only is breakfast good for your physical health, it is also a good time to connect socially. Even five minutes of talking with your kids or spouse while eating a quick bowl of oatmeal can boost your spirits before heading out the door.26

The last sentence of that quote is the most important. The overall advantage of getting up earlier is that we have more options. We can then use those options to better connect with the *people* God brings our way, beginning at the breakfast table.

One way to focus more on people is to use paper plates and disposable cups and bowls at breakfast. We use them for 99.9% of the meals at our house. That's because I refuse to work for $2.40 per hour. Let me explain.

When you use a washable plate you will spend 30 seconds scraping it clean, washing it, rinsing it, drying it and putting it away. That means you'll wash about 120 plates per hour. Paper plates can be purchased in bulk for 2 cents each and thrown away instantly. If you do that 120 times, you just saved an hour of work and it only cost you $2.40. Plus you eliminated the clutter of dirty dishes and squabbles over who would wash them. When you buy a paper plate, you are actually buying time.[27]

Let your quest for a streamlined morning routine be done in the right spirit, not like the efficiency expert who concluded his lecture to a group of businessmen with a note of caution, warning them,

> "You don't want to try these techniques at home."

> "Why not?" asked somebody from the audience.

> "I watched my wife's routine at breakfast for years," the expert explained. "She made lots of trips between the refrigerator, stove, table and cabinets, often carrying a single item at a time. One day I told her, 'Dear, why don't you try carrying several things at once?'"

> "Did it save time?" the guy in the audience asked.

> "Actually, yes," replied the expert. "It used to take *her* 20 minutes to make breakfast. Now *I* do it in seven."

Just doing things more efficiently, while not connecting with *people*, doesn't make for good time management. I have 12 children and I teach time management for a living, but I really don't carry a stop watch to the breakfast table like Mr. Gilbreth in "Cheaper by the Dozen."

Perking Potent Potions Produces Perky People

If the goal of breakfast is to connect with people and generate momentum, a good morning coffee can help with both objectives. Once we smell the aroma it's hard for us coffee drinkers to go back to sleep. Still, you may wish to save your caffeine jolt for later at work when you really need it.

If you want the best of both, try a decaf at home for aroma and warm fuzzies. Then, have the real thing a few hours later at work when you need the energy boost. I'll say more about that strategy in Chapter 8 on workplace momentum.

The only option I would discourage is the drive thru coffee shop on the way to work. Just do the math. A $3 per workday designer coffee habit costs $750 per year. Invest that amount in an IRA gaining 8% for 40 years and you could retire with almost $300,000 extra.

It's All About the Momentum

Again, we are not simply striving to trim the extra 30 seconds from the shower or calculate how to shave with the fewest strokes just for its own sake. Some might legitimately argue such a focus to be petty. Rather, we are streamlining our routines as a method of generating some useful momentum for the day.

When an airplane stalls it falls. Likewise, when we lose momentum through an ill planned morning routine, we stall, fall, and in some cases, we even crash and burn.

Everyone's morning routine is different, so I can't be as specific here as I would like. But with these principles and the motivation they produce, I believe you can ask God, and He will show you how to transform your ruts into routines that get you out the door with the morning momentum you desire and require!

Action Points

- Your perception of how long 5 minutes is depends on which side of the bathroom door you are on. If you have more people than bathrooms, consider officially scheduling morning bathroom time for greater family harmony.
- Set your phone or other timer to beep at set target times through the morning such as a two minute warning till the bus arrives.
- Put as many decisions on autopilot as possible. Prearrange who is going to let the dog out and when.
- Gradually acclimate to a lower shower temperature. Colder water wakes you up faster and saves money.
- Strive not necessarily for the fastest pace but the optimal pace. A winning marathon runner paces himself to avoid both running out of energy before crossing the finish line and crossing the finish line with energy to spare. It is no nobler to burn out than to rust out if burnout could have been avoided.
- Come up with happy momentum generators that work for you and your personality. Try singing, skipping, or laughing. Sing breakfast instructions opera style. Make a game of it and have fun!

Chapter 4

Planning Your Day

A young man applied for a job with NASA. The interviewer began, "Tell me young man, if we were to hire you, what would be your career goal with the space agency?"

"I've been thinking about that." He replied. "I want to become the first person ever to land on the sun."

"You want to land on the sun?" The astonished interviewer shot back. "Don't you know that if you were to land on the sun you would be instantly incinerated?"

"Oh I've been thinking about that too." He answered, "We'll need to make this a night mission."

I think you would agree, this young man was not cut out to be an astronaut. But he could still do just fine with time management, because time management is not rocket science. It is actually quite simple.

Roughly 14.2 trillion time management resources have been created over the past 50 years, with each one claiming to have discovered the "hidden secret" to managing time, which can only be known by purchasing their resource. Since you've already bought my book, and I don't have an "advanced course" to enroll you in for an additional fee, I'm going to go ahead and give you the bottom line to every one of those 14.2 trillion resources.

Time management has three simple steps.

Step One: Written Goals

You can't effectively plan your *day* unless you have first taken time to plan your *life*. Without long term goals, your life has no real destination. It is pointless to talk about routing today's segment of the journey until you've articulated where you want to end up.

Daily planning begins with a set of written long term goals. The first emphasis here is on "*written*." Until your goals are in writing they are simply wishes, and wishes generally don't come true. Writing crystalizes your thinking on what you desire to accomplish with your life. Time management expert Alan Lakein puts it this way:[28]

> *Planning is bringing the future into the present so you can do something about it now.*

The second requirement for our initial set of goals is that they be long term. The further into the future your goals reach, the more significance they take on. Most people's lives lack significance because they are planning for a lunch time instead of a life time. They are short term thinkers. They put more planning into the wedding than the marriage. They plan far more for summer vacation than for eternity.

Your plan must not only be written and long term, but it must also be done NOW. Procrastination is the ruination of your determination. I've probably not told you anything yet in this chapter that you haven't already heard several times. Everyone over the age of 12 knows they need long term written goals. Yet only about 3% of us ever take the time to write out exactly what it is we are trying to accomplish in life. The other 97% think it's a good thing to do, they just "already have too much on their plate for today, blah, blah, blah." If time is money, they are always broke, living paycheck to paycheck, because there has never been a good time to start investing for the future.

You are going to join that top 3% of highly productive people right now. I want you to set this book down, get a pen or keyboard in hand, and in 12 minutes or less, list five things you believe God wants you to do before you die. I emphasize limiting it to 12 minutes so you will go ahead and do it now. You won't get it perfect the first time, but that's OK. It is easier to edit than to create. You are writing them on paper, not carving them in stone. They can and will change with time, but the key is to start *now*, not "*someday* when you have time to really do it right."

Hit the "Pause Button" now till your list is complete.

Step Two: Prioritize Your Goals

Your next step is to attach a comparative value to each goal by ranking them in order of importance. Ask, "If I could only do one thing on this list, which one would it be?" Beside that item place a "#1". If you could only do one more, place a "#2" beside it, and so on down the list.

This is a critical step, because the essence of effective time management is to survey life's many options, identify the ones with the highest payoff, and then arrange your time to accomplish those most vital goals.

It is important to understand that goal setting for the Christian is fundamentally different from the world's approach. If you have ever taken a time management course in your workplace, the instructor probably began as I just did by saying, "Let's start with a set of goals." He or she then instructed you to create a "bucket list" of the things that will bring *you* the greatest pleasure. They advise, "Identify what *you* want from life." "It's all about *you!*"

But as a follower of Christ, goal setting is not "all about me." It's not just a matter of *inventing* my own goals. Rather, it is a matter of *detecting* what goals God has already established for me. That is an important distinction to make and one that shifts the direction from which we approach these first two steps.

With the big picture of your lifetime goals now in place, you will continue to set goals and prioritize at different intervals. I recommend that each year, on either New Year's Day or your birthday, you create yearly goals which advance you toward your lifetime goals, again with a prioritized ranking of each item.

Place these two lists, your lifetime and yearly goals, in a prominent place, like your physical desktop or computer desktop. This keeps them visible and relevant. They are your compass, establishing direction for your life. They supply the "why" which fuels the vision you will need get up and moving on mornings when you just don't feel like it.

Optionally, you may wish to create monthly and/or weekly lists of prioritized goals. These continue the process of vision casting and mapping out what we need to do *now* to experience God's best in the future. These medium range goals keep bringing the big picture into focus by breaking it down to doable tasks, in preparation for step three.

Step 3: The Daily Agenda

The final step is to create a daily agenda, using your medium and long range goals for reference points. Do this by listing all the things you need to do today, keeping your bigger goals in mind. Once these activities are determined, you apply the "Big Rocks First" principle.

It's become the most well-known illustration in the field of time management because it is a simple, visual object lesson of how to create a daily schedule. If it's new to you, or you need a refresher, it goes like this:

I, as the presenter, place a wide mouth jar on a table with about five large rocks, which I begin placing in the jar one at a time. I ask the audience to tell me when the jar is full. After about the fourth rock, someone says it's now full.

I reply, "It looks full. But, I also have a bucket of gravel under the table, which I'm going to pour over the big rocks." I fill the jar the second time, filling the space between the big rocks with gravel, and again ask "Is it full?" Some nod yes, others no. Then I repeat the process again, filling the jar with sand and finally with water until it really is full.

One person was asked if she understood what this had to do with planning a daily agenda. She replied, "Sure, I get it. It means no matter how full you day is, you can always cram in one more thing!" Sorry, that's not the point.

The point is, if I had started by putting the water, sand and gravel in first, could I have then gone back and put the big rocks in? No. The big rocks have to go in first or they never fit. They get crowded out by all the "little stuff" that went in first. But when the big rocks go in first, it's surprising how much little stuff can fit in around them.

Now let's go back to our list of activities for the day. Reflect on your long term goals. Then identify the #1 most important item on today's list and place it on the schedule first thing in the morning. Then, as much as possible, try to complete that activity before moving to #2 and continue to work your way down the list accomplishing items in priority order without skipping around.

A Cure for Frustration

Many people habitually go to bed exhausted after a very busy day, filled with activity, only to experience a sinking feeling deep in the pit of their stomach. It's a sense of quiet desperation, a feeling that somehow, "I missed it today. I didn't get it all done."

That happens because we begin our day with a list of 10 things to do. It may or may not be a written list, but we have ten things in mind for the day, two of which are very important. But because we aren't working off a prioritized agenda, we begin our morning thinking, "I'll start with #8 and get it out of the way so I can get really focused on #1." But #8 takes longer than we planned. Now its midmorning and we think, "I'll get #9 done while I'm in the mood for it." We continue this rationalization, filling our day with low priority activities, working from the bottom up. Bedtime comes. We are exhausted, and #1 and #2 are still hanging over our heads.

Now, let's reverse that process by starting at the top of the list and working down. We probably still won't get all 10 items done. Maybe only five. But that's OK. We couldn't have accomplished all 10 using any other method either. But this way we did the most important things, the things we determined were God's priorities for the day. Now if the anxiety comes, we can reject it as being from Satan and we can enjoy our rest, knowing we've done God's will that day.

It's Simple and It Works

Fred ordered a roach extermination kit advertised as "Guaranteed to work when you follow 3 simple steps." When the package arrived he opened it to find 2 wooden blocks and instructions for the three simple steps:

1.   Catch roach
2.   Place roach on block A
3.   Smash roach with block B

Well, not everything that is simple works. But when *God* gives a simple formula for planning.a successful day, we know it *will* work because God's way is the best way.[29] The big rocks first formula works, not because a modern time management guru cooked it up. It works because it's based in Scripture. Jesus said:

Seek first the Kingdom of God and His righteousness and all these things shall be added unto you.
-Matthew 6:33

Jesus spelled out for us what two of the big rocks were:

1. The Kingdom of God. (God working *through* me to build His Kingdom)
2. His righteousness. (God working *in* me to perfect His character in my life)

He said seek in these two areas FIRST. Then He promised to facilitate the other things (gravel, sand and water) as He sees we need them.

In the next chapter, we'll explore ways to apply this principle where the rubber meets the road, by seeking God during morning prime time.

Planning Quotes

- Either you run the day, or the day runs you. –Jim Rohn
- Nobody plans to fail, but most people fail to plan.
- A good plan violently executed now is better than a perfect plan executed next week. –George Patton
- Plan your work for today and every day, then work your plan. -Margaret Thatcher

- Reduce your plan to writing. The moment you complete this, you will have definitely given concrete form to the intangible desire. - Napoleon Hill

- The key is not to prioritize what's on your schedule, but to schedule your priorities. -Stephen Covey

Chapter 5

Meaningful Morning Devotions

Job was a godly man who enjoyed his morning time with the Lord. But he was also the owner of the largest business in the county and a father of ten.[30] With all those responsibilities there were surely mornings when unexpected situations popped up, disrupting his well-planned morning routine. Job then had to choose between his Bible and his breakfast before starting work. Anticipating that would happen, he predetermined which appetite would be fed first. He knew God wanted to "visit him every morning," so he declared, "I have esteemed the words of his mouth more than my necessary food."[31]

Most of us are just the opposite. Missing a meal is such a rare event we make sure everyone knows about it, *"I was so busy I didn't even have time to eat!!!"* Furthermore, missing breakfast makes us feel abnormal. As the day goes on, our stomach sends an intensifying message that something important is missing, until finally we prioritize food over whatever else has been clamoring for our attention. But when we miss morning devotions, does it create that same anxiety and spiritual hunger?

If you are alive (physically or spiritually), you will have *some* appetite. There's an impulse that says, "I need to eat." You have three options for responding to that impulse:

1. Ignore it and it will eventually go away after you starve to death.
2. Feed it with junk food to get immediate relief.
3. Strive to find the healthiest option time will allow.

It's easy to recognize the right choice, but healthy eating habits don't occur by default. They have to be cultivated and cultivation requires a systematic approach. That's why I'll spend the rest of this chapter presenting a smorgasbord of ideas to choose from as you cultivate a healthy spiritual breakfast habit into your morning routine.

Don't Even Think About Trying This!

Let's start with where to go, or maybe where *not* to go for devotions. The surest way to torpedo your morning quiet time is to rationalize studying your Bible in bed. If you've ever tried that, you know the only thing you will study is the back side of your eyelids. Quality time with God depends on being awake enough to hear His voice. He's been up all night waiting to spend time with you, so don't disappoint Him.

The goal of morning devotions is more than just staying awake, but staying awake is prerequisite to everything else. Until you do that, it is impossible to go to the next level of actually hearing from your Heavenly Father. Beyond the obvious step of getting out of bed, here are some more tactics for staying alert:

- Have a "stand up" meeting with God. Stand up meetings have gained popularity in the workplace as management has realized that standing keeps us focused and to the point.[32]
- Walk. Don't just stand, but walk around the room as you pray or read.
- Do your thinking on paper. Take notes, write, and highlight. Do something to interact with the text. The devil loves to send wandering thoughts when you are unprepared or passive in your devotion.
- Have a place you organize and store your insights such as a paper journal or notebook, or an electronic filing system like Evernote or OneNote. Even if you never refer back to them, just creating them will help you engage and get your mind around what God is showing you.

- Get your coffee first. While I do try to practice "Bible before breakfast" I will make an exception for some liquid sunshine. More about morning coffee strategies in the next chapter.
- Get comfortable, but not too comfortable. Think desk or kitchen table, not living room sofa or recliner.
- Speak. Talk out loud to God as you pray. The Bible speaks of how powerful the tongue can be for good.[33]
- Read aloud. Much scripture was originally written to be read aloud. The churches who received the original letters from Paul included many people who were illiterate and had to listen to it being read by others.[34]
- Try the different postures and positions mentioned in the Bible for prayer such as kneeling, falling on your face or raising your hands toward Heaven.
- Follow the example of Jesus and pray with your eyes open.[35]
- Remember your *first* goal is to get fully awake. Your second goal is to spend time with God.

When to Meet with God

Scripture teaches giving God the "first fruits" as the starting place for Biblical money management.[36] But I believe it also applies to time management. As we discovered in the previous chapter, seeking God is a "big rock" that has to come first, or it never seems to fit in. As a rule, getting your devotions in the soonest possible slot after you are dressed and alert is the best strategy.

Let's use another food analogy. Not giving God the first fruits means we are leaving Him our leftovers. Maybe you've had the experience of opening the refrigerator and seeing something green. The problem is it wasn't green when you put it in there. It is a leftover, and leftovers are always lesser quality than first servings. Sometimes we even feed them to the dog. Doesn't God deserve better than that?

Rising early to meet God may require a sacrifice on your part. If it does, you will be in good company. King David wrote, "*O God, thou art my God, early will I seek thee.*" He also said he would not make an offering to the Lord "*of that which cost me nothing.*"[37] Surely God is pleased when we love Him enough to "sacrifice" a few extra minutes of sleep to spend time with Him!

The Meeting Agenda

Every important meeting has an agenda. It gives guidance to the meeting and keeps things focused, productive and on topic. That doesn't mean we can't deviate or adapt as needed, but having an agenda does give structure and a starting point for discussion. Here are four items you might include on your morning agenda with God:

1. **Prayer**- This is simply talking to God and letting Him speak to you. If you have trouble getting started, here's a simple, well-known acronym, ACTS, you can follow:

    Adoration- Begin by adoring God in the beauty of his holiness.

    Confession- Tell God your failures and ask for His grace to forgive and to overcome.

    Thanksgiving- Dispel bad moods and overcome negative thoughts when you start your day by counting your blessings.

    Supplication- This means presenting your needs to God.

2. **Reading**- Read your Bible. Read a daily devotional book. Read after deeper Christian writers from past generations. There is a place for milk and for meat. There are a number of good websites and apps with customizable Bible reading plans. Ask a friend or pastor what they use. They'll be eager to demonstrate it!

3. **Meditation**- The word "success" is only used one time in all the Bible. It is promised to those who "meditate" on God's word[38]. That doesn't mean sitting in a yoga position and waiting for something mystical to happen. It comes from the same word as "rumination." That's what a cow does when it digests its food by chewing the cud over and over. We mediate by exploring original languages, and digging deeper with commentaries, Bible dictionaries and other Bible study tools.

4. **Action Points**- If spending time with God produces anything, it should give you direction for the day. I like to have my Bible on one screen and my daily planner on another. Planning time and devotion time should overlap and integrate. Perhaps God will bring someone to mind who needs your encouragement that day.

The Goal of the Meeting

Every meeting has not only an agenda, but a desired outcome or purpose it is intended to achieve. Whenever you read a book or article about prayer, one name always comes up as an example of a great man of prayer. George Mueller was a 19th century man of God who prayed in supplies for his British orphanages and saw many other miracles in direct answer to prayer.

In his autobiography he tells the goal of his morning time with God:

"I saw more clearly than ever, that the first great and primary business to which I ought to attend every day was, to have my soul happy in the Lord. The first thing to be concerned about was not, how much I might serve the Lord, how I might glorify the Lord; but how I might get my soul into a happy state, and how my inner man might be nourished. For I might seek to set the truth before the unconverted, I might seek to benefit believers, I might seek to relieve the distressed ... and yet, not being happy in the Lord, and not being nourished and

strengthened in my inner man day by day, all this might not be attended to in a right spirit …"[39]

How Long to Meet

Well planned meetings have not only a start time, but also a stopping time. I find it better to set a minimum *time* for devotions than a minimum number of chapters or pages. There is less temptation to rush through and "just get it done." You won't be tempted to read all two verses of Psalm 117 again just so you've read "a chapter."

I can't say what that minimum time should be for you, but consider this: How likely is it that you will come to the end of the day, lie down in bed and think, "I wish I hadn't spent so much time in prayer this morning."? For most of us that is not very likely. Be even more forward thinking and ask, "If I continue as I am, how likely is it that I will reach the end of my life and regret having spent too much time seeking God?" Again, for most of us that is quite unlikely. Give God the benefit of the doubt when in question.

Would you say someone who watches 35 minutes of TV each week *worships* TV? Probably not. Their lack of interest in TV would be evidenced by the fact they only give five minutes a day to TV.

Five minutes may be a minimum starting place to commit to spend with God, but seek to go up from there. As a special offering, try scheduling a day every so often when you rise extra early just to spend time with your Heavenly Father. Jesus did this.[40]

Years ago, parenting "experts" argued about which was needed, quality time or quantity time. Finally, I think they've figured out it takes both to develop and maintain a healthy relationship.

Get Your Priorities Right!

When someone says "I don't have time for that." What they are really saying is, "That is not a priority for me." They are saying, "I've chosen to do other things instead that are more important to me."

The truth is, since this time yesterday you've had the same 24 hours as every other person on the planet. If you haven't read your Bible or prayed, it is because you chose something else instead to fill those hours. That "something else" took priority over hearing from God.

If that is your struggle, you may appreciate this little poem called "*The Difference*"[41]

> *I got up early one morning and rushed right into the day;*
> *I had so much to accomplish that I didn't have time to pray.*
>
> *Problems just tumbled about me,*
> *And heavier came each task,*
> *"Why doesn't God help me?" I wondered.*
> *He answered, "You didn't ask."*
>
> *I wanted to see joy and beauty,*
> *But the day toiled on gray and bleak;*
> *I wondered why God didn't show me;*
> *He said, "But you didn't seek."*
>
> *I tried to come into God's presence;*
> *I used all my keys at the lock;*
> *God gently and lovingly chided,*
> *"My child, you didn't knock."*
>
> *I woke up early this morning, and paused before entering the day;*
> *I had so much to accomplish that I had to take time to pray.*

Take Action

You just invested several minutes of valuable time reading in this chapter. Now it's time for some tangible results. Don't be passive. Fill in this blank right now:

I will spend at least _____ minutes with God tomorrow morning.

Chapter 6

The Morning Commute

There is a wrong way, a right way, and an uncommonly excellent way to do anything, including our morning commute.

For many of us, that is a significant chunk of time. A recent Gallup poll found the average commute time in the US is 46 minutes round trip, with significantly higher times in some cities.[42] When you factor out those who indicated a "zero commute time," it's probably safe to say we average an hour a day getting from the front door to the desk and back. That translates into 250 hours per year getting to and from work. That's too big of a chunk of your life to simply drift through with no strategy for redeeming the time along the way!

Our commute time strategy is twofold: *Minimize* and *maximize*. We want to minimize the amount of time we spend traveling, while maximizing, or making the best use of, the time we do spend commuting.

The Solo Commute

86% of us commute to work in the car and 76% do it alone.[43] The game plan for keeping your morning momentum through a solo commute is to find creative ways to safely multitask. I emphasize the word "safely," because nothing is more important than keeping your vehicle between the ditches! John Wesley, the 18th century preacher who founded Methodism, was perhaps history's greatest example of a Christian who was careful with his time. He maximized his commute time by taking naps on horseback en route to his meetings. That specific type of multitasking might not be the safest practice while driving to work! Don't be like the pilot who, after a rough landing, announced to his passengers, "Sorry about that, folks. I was texting."

Multitasking while driving must be limited to activity that doesn't take your eyes off the road. That means using your *ears, mouth,* and *mind*.

Use Your Ears

Radio. If your community is blessed with Christian radio, take advantage of it by being more than a passive listener. Use the news stories not as a source for worry, but as promptings to prayer and action for the many needs you learn of. Let the story of a tragic house fire in your city become an opportunity to pray for, and give to, the homeless and afflicted in your home town. The key is to constantly think, "What action can I take as a result of what I am hearing?"

Education. Over time, you can self-educate a volume of knowledge equivalent of a university degree by making deliberate, focused choices of listening material for your commute. The possibilities are numerous:

- Sharpen your financial skills
- Learn negotiation tactics
- Perfect your time management skills
- Study history
- Improve your vocabulary with word building programs

Your public library probably has a great collection of CD's and possibly downloadable audio. Buying your own can be expensive, but it doesn't have to be. You can often get a $100 audio resource on EBay for $15. If you can get even one useful idea per day, it's well worth it. You're not just spending money; you are making an investment in yourself. Leaders are readers, or in this case, listeners. 63% of the wealthy listen to audio books during their commute to work vs. 5% of poor people.[44]

Foreign Language. One of the most rewarding skills is the ability to communicate with people in their own language. Despite the publisher's advertising claims, you won't totally master a new language this way, but it's a great supplement. I've learned much of my second languages, Spanish and Czech, by listening to audio in the car. I even learned one phrase in French. I can say, "Cut the grass." In French that's, "Mow de lawn."

Church Resources. Our knowledge is generally in an inverse relationship to its usefulness. That is, we know a lot about things that matter little and we know very little about things that matter a lot. Some men can rattle off all the latest statistics in their favorite sport, but they've never cracked a single book on how to be a better father. Some women know all the latest Hollywood gossip, but ask them what a person needs to do to go to Heaven, and they are clueless.

You can be different. Larger churches in your community often have vastly underused libraries with excellent audio resources on living the Christian life and finding answers to life's most important questions. They are generally happy to loan them to non-members as well.

MP3s/ Podcasts. Today as never before, we have the opportunity to become specialists in our trade or calling by simply being selective in what we listen to. A fifteen-minute internet search might yield several podcasts in your field of interest. Attending trade shows and conventions is expensive and time consuming, but nearly every convention I've spoken for makes the sessions available as an audio resource after the event for a fraction of the cost of attending in person. Of course, borrowing a set from your buddy who attended is even cheaper!

Audio Books. Entire books from both Christian and secular publishers are often available as audio resources. Some may be abridged versions of the printed original, which is fine. That simply means they have thrown out the bones and are giving you just the meat, which makes listening to it an even better use of your time. Here are some sources:

- MoodyAudio.com
- Audible.com
- ChristianAudio.com

The number one best seller of all time is also available as a free audio download in MP3 or as a free app. Listening to the Bible 15 minutes each day will allow you to take in the whole Bible in a year.

As you listen to these thought-provoking resources, applications of what you are hearing will come to mind. Someone said the most powerful nation in the world is the IMAGI-nation. Be ready to capture powerful new insights with the voice memo feature on your phone. You could also call your own phone and leave yourself a voicemail before you lose the thought, that is, as long as you can do so safely, which brings us to an important question:

Use Your Mouth

Is It Ever Acceptable to Use a Phone While Driving? This is a question some people feel quite strongly about. I've spoken to some who can't imagine how anyone claiming to be a Christian could talk on a phone while driving. Others would go into panic mode if they accidently left home without their phone. Whenever we feel strongly about something there is the tendency to get out of balance in our position and feel those who don't see it our way are being unreasonable.

If you are a 16-year-old who just got your license and you are driving on an icy mountain road on a foggy night through a construction zone in front of an elementary school which is hosting an all-night blind and deaf children's convention and the children are on unsupervised recess, you need to hang up and drive. If you are 40 years old, driving down an interstate highway in Montana on a sunny day with no other vehicle in sight, and your biggest danger is falling asleep from boredom, you are probably safe to make a call to your elderly mother on your hands-free phone.

Since real life situations fall between those extremes, our thinking on the subject should fall between extremes as well. Some professional people schedule calls during the morning commute, just as they would schedule them from the office, in order to get a jump on the day's work. Others keep in touch with extended family through regular commute calls. The bottom line is: use good judgment and a hands free phone, and always err on the side of safety.

Talk to God. Maybe you've heard the phrase, "He's so heavenly minded he's no earthly good." I suppose, at least in theory, it is possible to become that way. But how many people do you know who really fall into that category? Very few of us are guilty of spending too much time in prayer. I think nearly all of us could benefit by becoming *more* heavenly minded, even during our drive time.

I've experienced some of my best communion with God by myself behind the wheel of a car. I recall a few years ago driving through an awe inspiring mountain gorge near Loveland, Colorado. As I marveled at the beauty and majesty of God's creation, I began to praise Him out loud and thank Him for His goodness! God met with me in an unusual way that day, as He has at other times when I've cried out to Him while driving.

The Bible makes many references to crying out to God with a loud voice:

- "Cry out and shout, O inhabitant of Zion, for great is the Holy One of Israel in your midst!" -Isaiah 12:6
- "And when the ark of the covenant of the LORD came into the camp, all Israel shouted so loudly that the earth shook." -1 Samuel 4:5 (I've had cars beside me at a stoplight shaking with a loud noise, but not from prayer!)

- "And one of them [lepers], when he saw that he was healed, returned, and with a loud voice glorified God." -Luke 17:15
- The word "loud" is used 22 times in the book of Revelation to describe end-time events, including the volume of the worship in God's presence.

You may find it awkward to cry out to God at home or in church because of the distraction you might bring to others, but in the car it's just you and God. Whether you prefer a "quiet time" or a "shouting time," take advantage of the sound-insulated atmosphere to make your car a mobile "prayer closet."

Use Your Mind

In addition to prayer, another great way to multitask on the solo commute is to think. I realize we're all thinking all the time, but the problem is, we usually don't think about what we are thinking about. We have never disciplined our minds to think by default on important matters. Our minds are lazy, and unfocused to begin with, and the omnipresence of electronic amusement further numbs and dumbs our brains.

Think about the word "amusement." The prefix "a" means "not," or "the opposite of." The root word "muse" means "to think." And the suffix "ment" means "a state of." So an amusement is that which puts us in "a state of not thinking."

I'm not saying there is no legitimate place for amusement, (though I do prefer *recreation*, which is "RE- creation"), but, by learning to think about what we are thinking about, we can avoid the temptation to simply be "amused" during our morning commute. God says to "gird up the loins of your mind."[45] That means training your mind to focus on solving the day's problems, discerning God's will for the day, or engaging in spiritual warfare to defeat the plans of the enemy for the day ahead.

Fragments

After Jesus feed the multitudes he ordered his disciples to, "gather up the fragments that remain, so that nothing is lost."[46] Jesus gave us an example of being careful to make full use of the resources He gave, right down to the "fragments."

Keep a list, either mentally or in writing, of things you can do with a time fragment, such as 60 seconds at a stop light. You could:

- Trim your fingernails
- Comb your hair
- Take a drink of water (we all know we don't drink enough water)
- Read, quote, or memorize a Scripture from a "promise box" kept within reach
- Straighten the mess in your glove box
- Gather up any trash you can reach
- Organize your coins and reload your car change holder
- Organize your wallet or purse
- Take a breath mint
- Stick your head out the door to see if your tires need air
- Check your appearance- zippers, buttons, buckles, teeth, and nose

What if you get distracted and don't notice the light change? Don't worry, someone has defined a millisecond as the amount of time between when your light changes and when the guy behind you starts honking. You'll know!

Share the Ride

Multitasking is the key to maximizing your commute time. But since there are only so many ways to safely multitask while driving, if you want more options you'll have to get yourself out of the driver's seat. If you are a passenger, you can call, text, read, write, answer email or do computer work while your partner drives. You can make your car a mobile office while cutting your travel expenses in half.

But there is another important benefit to ride sharing. Years ago I heard a simple little statement that has been my guide for many decisions, large and small, ever since.

God's will involves people.

God is not as concerned with your efficiency at multitasking, as He is with your availability for Him to speak through you into someone's life. Sharing rides opens another avenue for building relationships with people. I've not been a regular commuter for several years, so I remember hardly any of the uneventful solo commutes I made back then. But I do remember the people I carpooled with 20 years ago. I especially remember those times when I shared the Gospel with my captive audience, or when I discussed the things of God with a fellow believer on our way to work. Few things are more satisfying than seeing God at work in your life before you even get to work.

Put up an offer to carpool on your bulletin board at work or on your social media. Ask God to set you up a divine appointment. Seek to have a Godly influence. God's will involves people.

The Family Commute

Perhaps you've heard about the new best seller for wealthy Christians. It's called "The Chauffeur-Driven Life." For many of us the idea of having a chauffeur would be a joke, but it might not be as unthinkable as you first imagine.

Wealthy people justify having someone drive them places on the basis that they can do something more valuable with their time than drive a car. And while your time may not have comparable dollar value to that of a Fortune 500 CEO, your time is still the most valuable resource you own. That's why if you have a teenage son or daughter, you might consider having them "chauffeur" you. Teens love to drive. And giving them the opportunity to do so under your supervision ensures they learn to do it right.

If you don't have a teen of your own and your hourly earning potential justifies it, you could even hire a neighborhood teen for minimum wage and still come out ahead, especially if you live in a city with express lanes for carpools.

Another strategy is to make the commute a time to talk with family. An August, 2005 story from Reuters News told about a man who stopped at a gas station in Italy. After his wife got out for the restroom without him noticing, he drove away. But what made the story newsworthy was the fact that he didn't notice she wasn't in the car until he was tracked down by police six hours later! He told the officers he hadn't noticed her missing because she always rode in the back seat with their little girl.[47]

I don't want to be too hard on this fellow. I'm sure he's already had a lot of explaining to do! But you can't help but wonder how someone could go six hours in a car and not speak to his spouse? Maybe it made international news because it's such an extreme example of a weakness many of us have: failure to communicate. Make it a habit to talk about meaningful things while traveling with family, such as on the way to drop off the kids for school.

Now that we've learned some ways to maximize our time in the car, let's find strategies to minimize the amount of time we spend commuting in the first place.

Traffic Tactics

You think your traffic situation is bad? It's probably mild if you compare it to the world's worst traffic jam which occurred April 12, 1990, as 18 million cars piled up along the East and West German border at the fall of communism. While you'll likely never be in a traffic mess like that, traffic, to some degree, is an inescapable part of the morning routine for most of us, and, projections show it worsening as our cities continue to grow. Short of moving, taking the train, or changing work, there really isn't a whole lot you can do to eliminate it. But there are some tactics smart people can use to escape any more traffic than necessary.

Avoidance. Unexpected traffic can sometimes be avoided by keeping your phone, tablet or GPS traffic feature turned on. You don't need a GPS to know how to get to work. But leave it on anyway as mapping apps are rapidly getting better at alerting motorists to traffic in more and more areas. Tablets allow you to easily scroll around to find the best alternate route. If you carpool, your partner can become your navigator. Now you have the justification for buying that new tablet you've been drooling over!

Eliminating Left Turns. UPS knows a thing or two about logistics. They have 95,000 big brown trucks delivering packages every day, so they've refined traffic navigation to a very precise science. Their hyper-efficient "package flow" software program maps routes for each of their drivers which reduce the number of left-hand turns. A UPS spokeswoman claims the software has saved them millions of gallons of fuel.[48]

Left turns require waiting for a clear spot in traffic going in and a clear spot in both lanes of traffic coming back out. Right turns only require an opening in one lane when returning to the road. When planning your errands consider making the stops on the right on your way to work and the stops on the left on your return.

Expedient Errands. If left turns and traffic are not a concern, I suggest doing all your errands on the way home instead of on the way to work. That way if something goes wrong, it won't put you in crisis mode. I remember once getting trapped in a fast food drive thru for about 30 minutes with no way to get out of the line. Had that happened on my way to work, the price of the burger would have gone up exponentially in induced stress.

More importantly, add to your spiritual momentum by thinking of ways to apply this verse to your morning commute:

In all your ways acknowledge Him, and He shall direct your paths. - Proverbs 3:6

God's will involves people. For example, you might think it saves time to always pay for your gas at the pump. But maybe you should occasionally go inside to pay, just so you can greet the clerks, smile and give them an invitation to church or a gospel tract. Most of the time I go inside the lobby at my bank, even though the drive thru might be quicker. I like for my banker to see me and remember me. I may need him some day!

Time Shift. Most traffic patterns are predictable. Schools and factories along your route start at the same time each day. Freeways slowdown about the same time every morning.

If you normally leave at 8:30 and poke through the next 30 minutes, perhaps you could leave 30 minutes earlier at 8:00, before heavy traffic, and be at work in 15 minutes. Now you leave home 30 minutes earlier but arrive 45 minutes earlier, creating 15 extra minutes.

Of course, this strategy only makes sense if you can either start your work 45 minutes earlier or do something else productive or enjoyable for 45 minutes until time to start work. Could you exercise or meet a co-worker for breakfast or Bible study? Experiment and see what happens.

Flex Time. There are 293 ways to make change for a dollar. That's a lot of different combinations! In the same way, there are many different combinations for working a 40 hour week.

Some jobs have to be 9-5, Monday through Friday. But if you have the option, experiment with alternate ways to arrive at 40 hours. Let's say you commute 30 minutes one way to work. If you work five 8-hour days, that's five hours a week coming and going. But, if you could accomplish the same thing by arriving an hour earlier and staying an hour later, you would work four 10 hours days and save an hour each week in commute time. That's 50 extra hours per year—or more than an entire work week!

Unlike asking for a raise, asking for a change in schedule isn't a request for more money from your employer. You don't know what they'll say unless you ask.

You may even be able to take it a step further and telecommute from your home office a few hours or days each week. If you are an information worker, present a "business plan" to your boss showing the advantages of allowing you a home work station. Make yourself available by being "on call" longer hours. Offer to take a 5% pay cut if they will just give it a trial run. You'll get their attention and, with the savings you gain in time and money by eliminating the commute, you may actually increase your net hourly wage.

Be a Contrarian

Getting out of the norm with your work and commute schedule is part of a broader strategy of being a contrarian. A contrarian is someone who does things contrary to the way most others do them. As Christians, this type of thinking should come naturally since God has told us not to be "conformed to this world."[49]

For example, where do you park when you get to work or when you go shopping? You probably snag the best place you can find, closest to the door. But you will likely save time by parking further away and walking a few extra spaces to the door. Consider the advantages of completing your morning commute with contrarian parking:

- You'll find a parking space quicker.
- You'll avoid congested areas near the entrance and lower the possibility of a bump up with a vehicle or pedestrian.

- You won't irritate others by holding up traffic in the parking lot waiting to claim your spot while someone is loading their stuff. (No one likes being "stalked" in a parking lot by someone wanting their space.)
- Your car is more visible, and thus more secure, when parked out by itself.
- There is less chance of a ding from someone opening their car door against your parked car.
- You have greater opportunity for exercise. The newest trend is special parking near the door for expectant mothers. Having had 12 babies ourselves, my wife and I were wondering: If they can't walk an extra 50 feet in the parking lot, are they really in any shape to be having a baby?
- You can easily back in or pull through so you don't have to back out at the end of the day when you are eager to get home.
- You show deference to those who may actually need a closer spot.

Jesus gave a stern warning to those who always grabbed the best seats at special gatherings.[50] I don't think it would be stretching things too far to apply the same principle to the modern parking lot.

God said His ways are not our ways.[51] That truth applies to more areas of life than most of us realize. As you purpose to take on new commuting habits, ask yourself questions like, "How would Jesus drive?" "Who would Jesus ride to work with?" "Where would Jesus park?" and, "How would Jesus respond to traffic?" Then, just try to imitate Jesus.

Key Points to Remember

- Strive both to minimize and maximize your commute.
- Use your ears, mouth and mind.
- Don't be so quick to dismiss mass transit if that is an option for you. Remember, God's will involves people.

- Allow enough margin to travel with calmness of spirit, even when there is a minor delay. It is not God's will for you to lose the spiritual momentum you gained from that morning's devotions during a harrowing commute.
- Bottom line: Commute like Jesus.

Chapter 7

Starting Your Workday

The manager of a classy restaurant stopped a scruffy looking man at the door and said, "Sorry pal, you can't come in here without a tie on." When the man returned from his pick-up with a set of jumper cables tied around his neck, the manager eyed him carefully and said, "OK. I'll let you in but just don't try to start anything."

The success of our workday hinges on how well we "start things" during the first hour. Nearly every effective business or ministry leader has developed tactics for a successful first hour, including the ability to dodge the many "weapons of mass distraction" they are ambushed with upon arrival at work. In this chapter we'll learn what those most productive first hour habits are, beginning with arrival time.[52]

Punctuality

Have you ever noticed how those who arrive late for a meeting are usually a lot more jolly about their tardiness than those who have been kept waiting? That's because those who habitually arrive late seldom realize the inconvenience their lack of punctuality causes others.

Some even glory in being "fashionably late." They never arrive on time because, in their small mind, a late arrival lets everyone else know they had more important things to do than to make the meeting on time like the "little people" do. Tardiness, however, is not a trademark of the important, but of the inconsiderate. And, if you are a salaried employee, expected on the job at a certain hour, late arrival means you are stealing from your employer.

Punctuality has been defined as "demonstrating the worth of people and time by arriving for appointments before they begin.[53]" I like that definition because it captures two key motivations to become punctual- a respect for time and thoughtfulness toward other people.

Research confirms the most successful people are those who apply the Biblical "extra mile" principle here.[54] They not only arrive at work on time, that's the minimum, but they build enough margin in their morning routine to arrive early.[55]

Who's in Control?

Perhaps the greatest benefit of arriving early is it puts you in control of your day, instead of the day controlling you. During the first hour you can see things more clearly. You can anticipate and prevent crises. You can identify your most important tasks and prioritize them before being bombarded with interruptions and trivialities. You can focus on people and relationships, not just projects and profits. We know, for example, that sending notes of encouragement and appreciation to customers and coworkers has a high payoff. But the reality is, once the phone starts ringing, it probably just won't happen.

Dealing with Interruptions

One of the quickest ways to lose control of your morning is the drop in visitor who stays too long. Without a tactic in place to dislodge them, they can quickly suck up all the margin and momentum you've worked so hard to create.

I heard one businessman share a tactic he found tactful, yet effective. When a guest stayed too long, he would say, "Come here, I want to show you something." He would then take them out of the office and show them something in the hallway. It could be anything, a plant, picture, or a gadget. It didn't matter as long as it was outside the office. Then he would excuse *himself* from them, which was much easier than telling them to leave his office.

A pastor friend of mine had a similar tactic. He said when he sensed a visit had gone long enough, he would say to the visitor, "Why don't we have a word of prayer before you go." As soon as he said the "Amen" he would rise and thank them for their visit as he walked them to the door.

You might think that sounds manipulative. But consider this fact. There is no such thing as an unimportant person. Every person is important to God and should be to us as well. But there are important people who will engage you in some very unimportant conversations if you don't have techniques in place for dealing with them.

Back to Work

Another tactic, which I learned from productivity expert Brian Tracey, is the simple three word phrase, "Back to work." When what started as a working conversation morphs into gossip, simply say, "I've got to get back to work." Say this phrase to yourself when you are tempted to open a frivolous email at work. It's great for keeping focus.

Be a Guest

You can often avoid the need for these tactics altogether by being the guest and not the host. Then, *you* decide when to arrive and when to leave. In many settings, "morning people" can save time by scheduling appointments early instead of later in the day when the other person's schedule is more likely to get backed up, causing you to have to wait to see them.

Group or committee meetings on the other hand may fit better in the afternoon. Many of us struggle to stay awake after lunch, making it a bad time to attempt creative work on our own. Doctors, for example, often schedule surgeries in the morning when their creative thinking skills are sharp, and schedule office visits in the afternoon. Ronald Reagan said, "I never drink coffee for lunch. I find it keeps me awake in the afternoon."[56]

Strategic Coffee Momentum

At least President Reagan was strategic about his coffee consumption. A book on morning momentum would not be complete without a strategy for what some folks consider their daily cup of "liquid sanity" or "fuel for the morning impaired."

I like coffee so much I once went 10 years without it. I had gotten to the place where I had to have a cup every morning, and often through the day, just to keep up to normal speed. What had started as an occasional boost for late night studies or early morning deskwork had become a dependency just to be "normal."

It was at that point I realized that I had crossed over the line the Apostle Paul warned of when he said, "All things are lawful for me, but all things are not helpful. All things are lawful for me, but I will not be brought under the power of any."[57]

After a 10 year coffee abstinence, our family took a four month long ministry trip (with all 10 kids!) to 30 countries of Europe and Africa to share our seminars. Knowing how important sharing a coffee is for fellowship in many cultures, and how much added energy I would need for such a trip, I started carefully indulging again. Today I'm still a coffee drinker, but I have coffee free Saturdays just to make sure it stays under control.

I don't know if coffee is good for your health or not. The "scientific answer" seems to depend on who is funding the study. But I do know it is a social drink that creates good synergy which makes people click in the workplace. Since we know that "God's best" plan for each day centers around people, it may be a good strategy to wait till work to enjoy your first cup with your coworkers.   A secondary benefit is that the delayed gratification of waiting till work will keep your coffee's addictive qualities in check.

Worst First

Another effective morning work strategy is the worst first tactic. In nearly every major work project, there is going to be one part we really don't want to do. It may be placing an unpleasant phone call, dealing with an unpleasant person or grasping some unfamiliar technology. Whatever it is, we will often procrastinate on that item, working all day under the cloud of the dreaded thing hanging over our head.

By doing the unpleasant thing first, we get it behind us quickly.   That generates excellent momentum by liberating us to now anticipate and enjoy the rest of the day. Some time management experts refer to this as eating a live frog. If you eat a live frog first thing each day, you will have a wonderful day, because the worst thing you have to do is now behind you. So learn to refer to your unpleasant task as your "live frog" and eat it early. If you have two frogs, eat the biggest one first.

Time Blocking

If your "frogs" generally take long to eat, you can benefit from "time blocking." The idea is to work in blocks of time for your most important projects so you can concentrate on them and finish them. Gary Keller explains benefits of morning time blocking in his book, *"The One Thing"*:

"Here's the productivity secret of this plan: when you spend the early hours energizing yourself, you get pulled through the rest of the day with little effort. You're not focused on having a perfect day all day, but on having an energized start to each day. If you can have a highly productive day till noon, the rest of the day falls easily into place. That's positive energy creating positive momentum. Structuring the early hours of each day is the simplest way to extraordinary results."[58]

When to Clean Your Desk

A common temptation when procrastinating on that unpleasant task is desk straightening. Shuffling paper is an effective way of pretending to accomplish something while really doing nothing. It deceives with instant gratification from seeing the "improvement."

We do need a time each day to straighten things. Unfortunately, that is also a time of vulnerability when we can be snared by piddling with the trivial instead of quickly delegating or eliminating it. The solution is to take away the incentive to piddle by saving desk straightening for the *end* of the workday. When all that stands between you and going home is some tidying up, you'll stay focused and buzz through it quickly. By leaving work with a clean desk, you'll be creating a "ready to go" environment for strong morning momentum upon arrival again tomorrow.

First Impressions Matter

First impressions are important. It has been said you never get a second chance to make a first impression. While that is true, you do get a new opportunity each morning to make a *daily* first impression by giving enthusiastic morning greetings to coworkers.

God wants us to make Him known in all our ways. To the extent we do, He promises to direct our paths.[59] Apply this promise when someone asks how you are, by saying, "I'm blessed" or "God's been good to me." I once knew a saintly older man who would enthusiastically reply "I'm as happy as a bumble bee in a clover patch, because I'm on my way to heaven!"[60]

Motivating others is like painting a fence. You can't do it without getting some "back splash" on yourself.

A Few More Quick Ways to Start Well

- Take the stairs. It's often faster than waiting for the elevator and the exercise gets fresh blood to your brain before you get trapped in your seat. Robert Frost said "The brain is a wonderful organ; it starts working the moment you get up in the morning and does not stop until you get into the office."
- Unless your work demands you do so, avoid the snare of checking email or social media first thing. You'll need some resolve to resist. The forces of habit and curiosity may seize you and pull on you stronger than a Pitt Bull on steroids.
- The first hour pace in some workplaces resembles a herd of turtles marching through peanut butter. Be a leader by striving early to set the right tempo for the day. It's contagious.
- Remember, quality time at work, quantity time at home
- Set the homepage and screen saver on your work computer to something that motivates but doesn't distract.
- It is more satisfying to start your day by doing something small on a high priority goal than by doing something big on a low priority goal.

Chapter 8

The Night Before

A Successful Morning Starts the Night Before

The most important factor to consistent early rising success is getting to bed on time. It is also the most difficult. That's why a successful plan to create morning momentum has to start with the previous evening. "Tomorrow" actually begins tonight.

The Biblical "day" begins, not with the rising of the sun, but with the setting of the sun. In the first five verses of Genesis, God tells how He created the world, starting with the night, and then creating the day. Verse five reads, "So the evening and the morning were the first day." Note He said "evening" first. This phrase is repeated five more times in the chapter as we are told "the evening and the morning" were the second through sixth days.

Whenever God says something over and over, it means He really wants us to get it. There are tons of hidden gems in Scripture for those willing to do some digging. Perhaps these verses have their application in how to think about the start of the day. For millenniums, the Jews have recognized the Sabbath as beginning at sundown Friday and continuing until sundown the next day.[61] I believe there is an application here for us as well.

Battles are often won or lost in the planning and preparation stage. Seizing your morning momentum is spiritual warfare and it's coming whether you are prepared or not. Two types of preparations are needed to get to bed on time and emerge a conqueror from the next morning's struggle. Prepare your stuff and prepare yourself. Let's look first at preparing your stuff.

Getting Stuff Ready

Backing In. Spell the word "stressed" backwards and you get desserts! I'm not sure there's a lot of significance to that, but perhaps reversing some routines would reverse some stress. One example is how we park the car.

Most people pull the car forward into the home driveway instead of backing in. But that is generally a short-sighted habit, because if you don't back in you'll have to back out. And it is usually more difficult to see the traffic when backing out from a driveway than when you are already on the road and can back in.

Backing in allows us to leave quickly if we're in a hurry. (Ever see a fire truck *not* backed in the station?) It shows more forethought and promotes readiness and momentum for the morning commute.

Clothing Chosen. The Bible gives several guidelines related to clothing including modesty, gender distinction, and economy.[62] But the one Jesus himself referred to was that we not be anxious over clothing.[63] He knew how much anxiety some of us would attach to what should be a minor concern.

Lower that anxiety by making clothing decisions the night before and laying the chosen garments out ahead of time.[64] This eliminates possible momentum loss from last minute, dirty, unironed or missing clothes. This is especially true with children. One of the devil's favorite tricks at our house is to hide children's shoes on Sunday mornings! We've largely defeated that tactic now by assembling the kid's clothes as little figures with shoes, pants, and shirt all in place on the sofa before going to bed. Someone walking in our home Saturday night would think the rapture had just taken place!

Pocket Stuff. When you prepare your clothes, do a quick inventory of your pocket contents. Do you have keys, comb, wallet, fully charged phone, pocket knife, change, and any other items you carry on your person? If something is missing, it's better to find out now. Establish your spot to store things. When in a hotel, I always put my pocket stuff on top of the TV. Put little stuff in your shoes. You won't miss anything that way.

Brief cases, purses, and backpacks all need a spot to call home too. You're more likely to stay faithful to your morning workout if the gym bag is packed and waiting for you.

Breakfast. There is no reason you can't decide the night before what tomorrow's breakfast will look like. You won't have any information in the morning you don't have already. Get the coffee pot ready to perk or invest in one with an automatic timer that fills the house with coffee aroma before you wake. Set the cereal and fruit out on the counter. Set the table. You will be more likely to think rationally and make better, more nutritious choices the night before, than in the heat of the battle during morning rush. The same applies with any packed lunches. Put them in backpacks along with school supplies, ready to grab and go on a peg or hook by the door.

Better yet, if you have children, delegate as many of these tasks as possible to them. We have a general rule in our home that a job goes to the youngest child capable of doing it. We've found children as young as three can sort silverware from the dishwasher and put away toys. All too often, we deny our children the opportunity to learn the character traits needed for future success when we don't train them to work at an early age.

Give them tools, not just toys. A 10 year old boy can get just as excited about a new tool set as he can about an electronic gadget, if his appetite for it is properly cultivated. The Bible says, "Even a child is known by his deeds, whether what he does is pure and right."[65] Make them part of your momentum building team.

Stuff Ya Gotta Do. Are you afraid you will forget something that "has to" be done before you go to bed? Got clothes to iron, email to answer, or a bill to pay? Place the item, or a reminder of the task, on your bed. That way it becomes impossible to overlook it or ignore it before going to bed.

Settling the Questions. Getting your stuff ready the night before is a key part of your strategy of having fewer decision points in your morning routine. You want your morning routine to be on autopilot as much as possible because every decision point brings a potential stumble to your momentum. Satan is constantly trying to get you off course by tempting you to take the path of least resistance at every fork in the road. Have it settled how many push-ups you'll need to do before breakfast and whether you really need all the calories you'll get from a second bagel with cream cheese. Proverbs warns us, "A prudent man foresees evil and hides himself, but the simple pass on and are punished."[66]

Preparing stuff the night before frees your mind the next morning to think on matters which require creative energy. Those are the activities which both generate and require morning momentum. During the evening, when your mind is tired, is often the better time to make lunches, select clothes, and do tasks which most anyone who has a pulse can do.

Getting Self Ready

Sundown finds many of us finishing the evening meal. That's a good transition point to start thinking about the next day. Do a quick, after-supper inventory of what you need to do to get yourself physically, mentally and spiritually ready for bed on time. One of those is brushing your teeth.

Cleaning the Choppers. Dentists now recommend waiting about 30 minutes after a meal before brushing.[67] That gives time for after dinner talk and cleaning up from supper. Then, go mop the molars. There are several advantages of brushing after dinner instead of waiting till bedtime:

- Fresh breath through the evening
- Better dental hygiene
- You'll be less likely to have an inappropriate "midnight snack"

But the big advantage of brushing early is the signal it sends your body and mind to start the transition toward bedtime. Switching your reference point forward toward bedtime creates momentum to get those "have to" tasks done sooner instead of later. Get them done and you'll feel free to enjoy some family time, recreation, or whatever event your evening holds, without worrying about getting to bed too late. At bedtime, take a quick swish of mouthwash. It prevents a demotivating sense of morning breath when you wake up.

Ready, Set, Go…to Bed

As bedtime approaches, try setting an opportunity clock (what we used to call an alarm clock) for bedtime, just as you do for wake up time. Any marksman will tell you it is harder to hit a moving target than a fixed one. Setting an alarm "fixes" bedtime in your mind and can even allow you to make a game of getting in bed before the alarm goes off!

One of the universal laws of time management is that work expands to fill the time allotted for it. Without a target bedtime there will always be one more thing that "has to be done" before we can get to bed. When we are operating under a deadline we are forced to prioritize and choose the most important things first to be sure they get done.

Another rule of time management is that everything takes longer than you think. So start preparing for morning early enough to include margin for a minor problem or two. If they pop up you'll be ready. If they don't, you've created some "bonus" time you can enjoy before going to sleep.

Do's and Don'ts

- Do turn off the TV your last half hour.
- Don't bring up stressful or controversial topics of conversation as bedtime approaches.
- Do a quick pick-up of things scattered around the house. That keeps you from being distracted by wanting to pick them up in the morning.
- Don't check email on your way to bed. It is a sure way to get sidetracked and stay up longer than you planned. It will still be there in the morning.
- Do as much as you can as early as you can. You'll be glad you did.
- Don't go to bed angry. God tells us to get issues resolved quickly and not to "let the sun go down on your wrath."[68]
- Do remember there will always be "One more thing" you *could* do. But not necessarily one more thing you *should* do.

Determining Your Bedtime

You will spend a third of your lifetime sleeping. That's more than any other single activity and a huge chunk of your life. Yet most of us who complain we "never have enough time" have never systematically determined the optimal amount of time we need to sleep.

Fortunately, we can benefit from the legacy of someone who was very methodical in his approach to rising and retiring. He was the founder of the "Methodist" church, John Wesley. The Methodists got their name from Wesley's methodical approach to Christian living. That approach included being very systematic in determining just how much sleep his body actually needed. Once he determined that amount, he simply did whatever was necessary to keep that schedule.

Wesley determined this by rising at the exact same time each morning and retiring at the exact same time each evening. Then, if he stayed awake more than a few moments after his head hit the pillow, he knew he had slept too late that morning. The following day he would adjust his rising time back until he fell asleep instantly that evening. By using this method he was able to sleep as much as needed but no more.

John Wesley devoted an entire sermon to this topic. I've translated that message into modern English, and added some of my own notes to it. It is available at LifeChangingSeminars.com. I encourage you to invest 15 minutes in reading his challenge and learning his method. The return on that 15 minute investment will be fabulous!

Redeeming the Time While You Sleep

You are finally in bed! There is only one more thing to do: Go to sleep. And like all other activities of your busy day, you can do it the way the masses of unthinking people do, or you can strive for excellence by doing it God's way.

Maybe you've seen a scary movie just before bedtime that gave you nightmares. That's because what we focus on as we fall asleep tends to guide our thoughts in the night. As computer programmers say, "Garbage in, garbage out." But the opposite is true as well. Put the good stuff in and you'll get good stuff out!

That's why God says to focus on His Word as we lie down at night.[69] By choosing a Scripture to think on as we fall asleep, we direct our nightly thought patterns to God.[70]

Another strategy is to ask God a question as we fall asleep and open our minds to hear his guiding voice in the night. David compares this do turning over our reins, like controls over a horse, to the Lord each evening:

> *I will bless the Lord, who hath given me counsel:*
> *my reins also instruct me in the night seasons.[71]*

Someone once made the profound observation that the best cure for insomnia is to just get some sleep. While that is true, I also believe sleeplessness is sometimes the result of preventable attacks from the enemy. If that is the case, Satan will flee when you practice these techniques. He would much rather have you sleeping than meditating on God's Word.

Mornings are Created Twice

Everything is created twice, once in the planning stage, and again in the execution stage. Your house was first created by an architect on his computer, then by a contractor with a hammer. Your car was first created by an engineer, then by a factory worker. Likewise, your morning has its first creation the night before.

Your first thought in the morning is spawned by your last thought at bedtime. Your morning momentum will be proportional to the anticipation you create for the next day at bedtime. Get some positive expectations for the day in mind at night and you won't have to drag yourself out of bed. You will be excited about getting out of bed!

A successful life is one with no regrets. That life materializes as we think far enough ahead to take steps *now* to avoid regrets *later*. When you wake up the next morning, you will seldom ever regret having gone to bed on time the night before. But you will often regret having stayed up too late the night before. You will seldom regret having skipped your "midnight snack" but you will often regret that late night cheeseburger that now feels like a rock in your stomach.

Delay gratification and engage in extra forethought during the time of first creation (the night before) and you will be initiating a superior plan for morning momentum. Begin with the end in mind, and you will create a day with no regrets.

Chapter 9

Follow Their Example

Follow Inspiring Examples

An aged, country farmer took his decrepit old mule to qualifying day at the Kentucky Derby. A taken back race official asked, "You mean you want to enter *him*?" The old-timer answered, "Well, I don't figure he can win, but I thought the association might could do him some good."

The farmer had the right idea. Those we associate with have a powerful influence on us. That is why wise people will seek out other wise people whose successful lives they can imitate and learn from. Proverbs, God's wisdom training manual, says, "He that walketh with wise men shall be wise"[72]

One way we can walk with the wise is to study the lives of wise people who have gone before us. Successful people leave behind clues to their success. As we examine the record, we see an undeniable, consistent pattern of successful people whose extraordinary momentum began each day with early rising.

Bible Patterns

The Bible is filled with examples of those who rose early, eager to seek God's best for the day ahead:

- **Job** was a man with great responsibilities who rose early in the morning to pray for his family.[73]
- **Gideon** needed God's instruction for a major decision, so he asked in faith for God's specific direction. He rose early in the morning in anticipation of God's response.[74]

- **Joshua** had been promised overcoming victory by God. It was his practice to rise up early to launch the battles he faced and claim the victory God wanted him to experience that day.[75]
- **Abraham** had to perform the extremely difficult task of sacrificing what he cherished most to the Lord. When the appointed day came, he rose early in the morning instead of procrastinating.[76]
- **Moses** had a very special message God wanted him to share with an important leader. He obeyed God's instruction to rise early, making sure his words would be exactly what God planned to communicate through him.[77]
- **Samuel** rose early to carry out God's instructions to anoint the ruler of a nation.[78]
- **King Darius**, though a heathen king, feared having offended "the living God" by putting Daniel in the lion's den. He rose early to witness a demonstration of the delivering power of the true God.[79]
- **King David** exhorted his people to meet God early in the morning.[80]
- **Jesus** got up "a great while before the day" to spend time with His Heavenly Father.[81]

It is also worth noting that the greatest event in the Bible, or in all history for that matter, occurred just as the first beam of sunlight began to break over the horizon.[82] God could have planned for the resurrection of Jesus to happen at any time of day. But He often orchestrates events as object lessons to illustrate deeper truths. Perhaps he chose the first moment of the new day to picture the optimal time for a new beginning.

But it's not just in the scriptures that we see God's blessing on those who sought Him early. All through history those who accomplished great things for God were the ones eager to get started while the contented multitudes languished in bed.

Historical Examples

John Wesley, whose "method" we learned in the previous chapter, was perhaps used of God more than any other individual since the Apostles to bring genuine revival in his day. From his conversion in 1738, until his death in 1791, Wesley preached 40,000 sermons, traveled more than 250,000 miles on horseback, published scores of writings, and shook two continents for Christ.

John Wesley gave his circuit rider preachers a book of 52 standard sermons as a basis for their training. One of those sermons was on the topic, "Redeeming the Time." What would such an ultra-high producer advise to be the most crucial discipline needed by those who would redeem the time for God?

Wesley's entire sermon was an exhortation to early rising. He rose consistently at 4:00, often preaching his first sermon at 5:00. It is also worth noting that he attributed his longevity to this practice.

Martin Luther lived in an era when very few people showed an interest in God's Word and the idea of "Morning devotions" as we know it would have been unknown. Yet he began his day by reciting the Ten Commandments, a creed, and The Lord's Prayer. If you know anything about church history, you know the result of those morning devotions.

George Mueller is a name synonymous with fervent, effective prayer. He had a lot to say about the value of meeting God before meeting anyone else. He wrote, *"How different it is when the soul is refreshed and made happy early in the morning, from what it is when the service, the trials, and the temptations of the day come upon one without such spiritual preparation."*[83]

"The Hand of the Diligent Maketh Rich" (Proverbs 10:4)

The Proverbs have a lot of good things to say about diligence and diligent people. One of the Hebrew words translated as "diligent" is "Shachar" which can mean "to be up early at a task."[84] We are told that diligent people will be blessed and promoted in various ways, often (but not always) including financial prosperity[85].

God paints a detailed illustration of diligence in the industrious woman of Proverbs 31. A list of her most outstanding character qualities includes "She riseth also while it is yet night."[86] The result is a family that is well provided for with enough left over to be a blessing to the poor.[87]

God's principles work when applied by non-believers as well as by Christians. Numerous studies have shown a direct correlation between a disciplined morning routine and career success:

- Dave Ramsey notes that 44% of the rich wake up three hours before work starts. Only 3% of the poor do so.[88]
- 76% of the wealthy exercise aerobically four days a week. 23% of the poor do this.
- 88% of the wealthy read 30 minutes or more each day for education or career reasons vs. only 2% of the poor.[89]
- A Harvard researcher discovered early risers were more proactive. They are more likely to anticipate problems and make plans to deal with them effectively, leading to more success in the business world.[90]

A Few More Samples

Maybe you heard of the little boy who woke up scared in the middle of the night calling for his father. His dad, in an attempt to calm him, reminded him that he didn't need to worry because his Heavenly Father was in the room with him. "I know that," the boy replied, "But I still need someone with skin on them."

Here are some examples of people who, Christians or not, illustrate the tangible rewards of morning momentum "in skin."

- **Benjamin Franklin** was perhaps the most prolific American in history. We know him as a founding father, inventor, author, publisher, diplomat, philosopher and scientist. But he was also the third richest man of his day. (If you want people to believe something, just tell them that Ben Franklin said it!) He really did say, "The early morning has gold in its mouth." He rose at 5 and went to bed at 10. He used the first three hours each day for reflection, preparation, breakfast and planning.
- **Margret Thatcher**, "The Iron Lady" was my favorite British politician. She was up every day at 5 a.m.
- **Frank Lloyd Wright** is a name synonymous with creativity and bringing a vision to life. He was up at 4.
- **GE CEO, Jeff Immelt**, gets up at 5:30 for a cardio workout during which he reads the papers and watches the news. He claims to have worked 100 hour weeks for 24 straight years. (Not recommended!)
- **GM CEO, Mary Barra**, is already in the office at 6, before most of us even get up.
- **Former PepsiCo CEO, Steve Reinemund**, ran four miles every morning at 5. It was the only way to be sure he would get his run in before getting caught up in corporate affairs. He is now dean of a business college where he invites students to join him for an early morning jog. He calls it "Dawn with the Dean."
- **Both Bush Presidents** were early at it. The first being up at 4 to go running and be in the office at 6. This was despite the fact he sometimes went to bed at 2. A former White House nurse who had to keep up with him said, "He was a horror." The second Bush held meetings in the White House starting at 6:45. Maybe that's why his Secretary of State, Condoleeza Rice, was up at 4:30.[91]

Bad Examples

A man complained to his buddy, "My life is useless. I'm a total failure." "Don't be so discouraged," chimed the friend. "You can always serve as a negative example for others."

God gives a number of negative examples of those who missed a blessing because of inappropriate sleep or a lack of discipline.

- **Jonah** was running from God when he was awakened by the words, "O sleeper, get up and call on your God"[92]
- **Samson** had a habit of sleeping at the wrong place at the wrong time. He paid dearly for it.[93]
- **Peter** succumbed to the temptation of sleep at prayer time. Soon afterwards he wept over his lack of spiritual stamina as he fell into the very temptation Jesus had alerted him to.[94]

Think of those you know who answer the door in their PJ's after rolling out of bed at the crack of noon. Are they the successful people you want to model your life after? In fact, can you think of a single example, in scripture or elsewhere, of someone whose life was characterized by laziness who ever amounted to anything?[95]

Ultramarathoners

A recent Time magazine article documented a unique group of athletes for whom running a marathon just isn't challenging enough. They are called "ultramarathoners" and they have trained their bodies to do amazing feats.

One 42 year old ultramarathoner has run 262 miles non-stop in 75 hours, mountain biked for 24 hours straight, ran 146 miles across Death Valley in the middle of summer, and swam across San Francisco Bay. Ultramarathoners must overcome pain, cramps, exhaustion, and vomiting. Yet they provide an amazing example of what endurance the human body is capable of with proper training and commitment.

When I read that article I thought, "What lengths am I willing to go to in order to achieve what God has called me to do?" One man in the article regularly rises at 2 a.m. and runs 50 miles. Am I willing to get up 15 minutes earlier to pray and plan?

Speaking of the elite athletes of his day, the Apostle Paul said, *"And everyone who competes for the prize is temperate in all things. Now they do it to obtain a perishable crown, but we for an imperishable crown."*[96] People who get excited about athletics are called "fans" and are generally viewed favorably by society. People who get excited about God are called "fanatics" and are generally viewed negatively by society.

You and I are in a race with time. We will be winners or losers for all eternity. Let's do whatever it takes, even if some think it "fanatic," to win this race.

Chapter 10

Special Situations

Gladys began a chat session with tech support. The agent wrote, "Click the start button on the left side of the screen." Gladys wrote back, "You mean on your left or mine?"

At least Gladys realized that people see things differently. Diversity in His children is evidence of God's creativity. That diversity means we won't all take the exact same approach to gaining morning momentum. One size doesn't fit all. So, let's adapt the principles we've learned to those with different circumstances.

Night Owls

The most common objection I hear when teaching the advantages of early rising is "But I'm not an early bird. I'm a night owl." My reply is that before we can confirm or deny the benefits of being a "night owl" we must define that term.

There is a big difference between an occasional late night of focused work on a vital project, and habitual late night TV and web surfing. The one is a deliberate, strategic tactic used by successful people. The other is the result of undisciplined rationalizations of the weak willed.

I hope you won't consider me a hypocrite if I confess that portions of this book extoling early rising were written in the middle of the night. I like to occasionally get a coffee with one of my teens at the local 24 hour restaurant around 11 p.m. and work there till 2 or 3 a.m. It is a deliberate, planned strategy for making memories and producing blocks of content. And that's OK.

Jesus is our example in all things. He stayed up all night on occasion in preparation for a special event. However, this was probably the exception and not the rule. As a matter of habit, few of us gravitate toward more focused and productive habits at night, when we are worn out from the day, than in the morning when we are fresh.

It is true some "night owls" appear to be productive people. But if they applied the principles we've learned in the first nine chapters, I can't help but wonder if those same "productive" people could become "super-productive" people. The data certainly suggests they could.

Students

There is probably no stage in life when being a night owl is more common than during our student days. "I work best under pressure" is the popular belief (or should I say rationalization?) of those who habitually cram for exams the night before. But does research support the notion that such procrastination enables a higher quality education?

In 2008, the University of Texas did some extensive research on this question involving over 800 students. The results were conclusive. Those who identified as early birds had grade point averages a full point higher than those who identified as night owls: 3.5 vs 2.5. The results held true even after researchers took into account other factors related to higher GPAs, such as SAT scores and other standardized tests that measure academic ability.

It's not hard to understand the "why" behind these results. Morning people find it much easier to get to class alert and on time. Staying up late exposes you to greater temptation from negative behaviors that will decrease your academic performance.[97] And, your brain is simply worn out at the end of the day. It doesn't absorb or process new information as well.

Perhaps Solomon observed a similar situation in his day when he wrote at the end of Ecclesiastes, "*And further, my son, be admonished by these. Of making many books there is no end, and much study is wearisome to the flesh.*"[98]

On Vacation

Pierre Beauchemin was the world's most flexible man. His unique ability to dislocate his leg joints allowed him to scratch his ears with his feet and turn his legs completely around so he could literally walk backwards. He could even fold himself up small enough to fit in a picnic basket.

Pierre was a good example of flexibility, which is the sensible approach to morning momentum during special events like vacation. A vacation is, by definition, a break from your normal routine. That means it's OK to stay up late making memories with the kids and sleep till 10:00 without guilt.

On extended vacations, I would also urge you consider at least one or two early mornings with God. Praying as you watch the sun appear over the horizon at the beach or the mountaintop resort, is thrilling to me. It is also one of the most rejuvenating methods of "getting away from it all."

Parents of Newborns

I once heard someone congratulate parents of a newborn with the cheer, "Let the sleep deprivation begin!" Though said as a joke, it reflected a truth. I love babies. That's why we've had 12 of them. But their sinful nature means they are actually very selfish little creatures that really don't care if they keep you up all night or not!

Your baby may be God's little alarm clock to awaken you for special prayer. The Bible speaks of a continuous spiritual warfare going on about us. If the devil is causing your baby to wake, try reading scripture in bed while getting them to sleep. Pray over your child. Sing and claim God's promises related to your baby. The devil would certainly rather have you asleep than causing him problems!

But, the Christian's ultimate defense for surviving those nights is understanding the sovereignty of God. By that I mean, keep in mind that God alone has the final say over when your baby sleeps and when she cries.

A few months ago I was awakened about 3 a.m. by a crying baby. When I went to her room, I picked up a faint smell of smoke. I then discovered a space heater had overloaded a circuit that was causing some wood paneling to smolder and was likely just minutes from catching fire. We had taken our smoke alarm down when someone made a burnt offering out of supper the night before and we had forgotten to put it back up. A crying baby likely saved our home from tragedy that night!

The psalmist reminds us,

"Out of the mouth of babes and nursing infants
You have ordained strength,
Because of Your enemies,
That You may silence the enemy and the avenger."[99]

Parents of School Age Kids

Strangers often see our large family in public and ask how we have such well-behaved children. My short answer is, "We don't give them any other options!" That is the same approach you may need with getting them up on time- "No other options." Your goal as a parent is to raise self-disciplined kids. But children rarely develop self-discipline on their own without some imposed discipline in the formative years.

Children are short term thinkers. They nearly always choose the path of least resistance, so creating an atmosphere where wake up time is non-optional won't always be fun. But the payoff will be lifelong for both of you. Some of my greatest joy has come from witnessing my two, early rising, adult girls recently answering the call of God to medical training to serve in whatever mission field He directs them.

Of course, non-optional doesn't mean we have to be negative about it. Try some cheerful music, like a John Phillips Souza march, to set an upbeat atmosphere. Give a special prize to the first one to the breakfast table. Everyone, including kids, can get up when they *want* to get up.

Finally, remember that getting them up on time requires getting them to bed on time. Every bedtime ritual you establish can come back to haunt you. Getting the kids to stay in their room can feel like playing Wack-A-Mole if you allow it to. Streamline and keep it simple.[100]

Travel Days

I can speak with a little authority on this topic having traveled to all 50 states with my family. We've also done our share of international travel, including a four month, 30 nation, trip to Europe and Africa a few years ago with 10 kids.[101]

I can honestly tell you that in all those miles of travel, my children have never had a backseat squabble, whined for a drink, or asked for frequent bathroom breaks. They have never done any of those things…as long as they have all been asleep.

That makes super early morning momentum especially powerful on travel days. Pack everything the night before, leave at 4 a.m. and you'll get 5 free hours of quiet travel before they even know what's going on!

On flying days I used to think it smart to time things so I could arrive at the gate just a few minutes before departure. That worked fine until one day I arrived late. When I bought my ticket, I had agreed with the airline that if they were ready to go and I wasn't there they could just go ahead and leave without me. They kept their part of the agreement! Now I arrive extra early and bring something productive to do in the gate area while I wait. It's a lot less stress.

Home Educators

Maybe you heard about the Washington bureaucrat who decreed farmers were no longer allowed to bail their hay in round bundles. He had determined cows needed three "square meals" per day. Like that bureaucrat, many of us are unthinkingly attached to the idea that we all need three square meals per day. But most of us can get by just fine on two.

One of the greatest advantages of home schooling is the flexibility of schedule. By having a later breakfast, around 10 a.m., and an earlier supper, our family has saved thousands of hours by not cooking, eating and cleaning up lunch. It also gives incentive for morning momentum when certain jobs or subjects have to be completed before you can eat breakfast.[102]

One challenge to momentum home schooling moms face is constant interruptions from little people during morning quiet time. You can solve this by making a "Blood & Smoke" rule. That means you are only allowed to interrupt Mommy for things involving blood or smoke. (Hopefully no one will have a heart attack as that would not qualify!)

My wife, Carrie, has a whole section of free time management resources in the home school section of LifeChangingSeminars.com. She has more ideas than Van Camp has pork & beans!

Working from Home

I love working from home because of the liberty it brings me. I would much rather make less money and have the freedom to set my own schedule. But greater liberty comes with a greater potential danger of abuse. That's why the Apostle Paul warned, "Use not your liberty as an opportunity for the flesh."[103]

One way to manage that liberty is to develop the work mentality of a "go to work-er" by setting a time each morning when you formally start work. Without target times for starting and stopping, your liberty can become a license to laziness. Or, on the other hand, without set hours, you may never be able to relax and know when you are truly "off the clock."

Sick and Tired

We all get sick at times, and there is such a thing as genuine physical exhaustion which we've all experienced. No one should feel guilty for taking additional rest during those times.

For those times when your body requires a season of extra rest, remember you can also add extra hours by going to bed early and taking afternoon naps, while continuing to reap the physical, mental and spiritual benefits of early rising. The Psalmist may have tried this approach when he cried,

I rise before the dawning of the morning,
And cry for help;
I hope in Your word.[104]

Depression

Those experiencing the pain of deep depression may find their only relief comes from crawling into bed as soon as possible and hiding there as long as possible. If that is you, there is no information in this book that can help you. That is because no amount of information will change a depressed person, only actions will.

The only way to end your emotional pain is by taking *action* first thing in the morning. You may still feel depressed even if you do wake up earlier. But it is vital that you seize the moment anyway. Exercise. Meet a friend for breakfast. Get out of bed and out of the house. Positive emotions will only flow from positive actions. Your *motions* control your *emotions*. You have nothing to lose by trying.[105]

Retired Folks

Scripture admonishes older saints to set the example for the rest of us.[106] I once attended a Florida church with a large retirement community. I was encouraged as a young person by the example of the senior saints there who gathered regularly for early morning prayer.

You may not be able to apply every concept in this book because of the limitations of age. But focus on what you *can* do, not what you *can't*. For example, If you physically can't do exercise in the morning, at least do some extended stretching. Even Friendly, my Golden Retriever, know that stretching presses sluggish blood through the body at a quickened pace allowing more of it to reach the brain, accelerating the wake up routine.

Wen Moses was 80, he likely thought all the big stuff that was going to happen in his life had already happened. But he was wrong. As he kept meeting God in the early mornings, he discovered the greatest exploits were yet to come![107]

Weekends

One of the most neglected commands in all Scripture is the Sabbath day principle. Our great grandfathers called it, "The Holy Sabbath." Our grandparents called it "The Sabbath." Our parents called it "Sunday." And we call it "The Weekend."

Most Christians today associate Sabbath observance with "legalism" and an irrelevant, negated Old Testament law. But the principle of one day of rest for every six days of work was established long before the law. God established the 1:6 ratio of work and rest in the creation week. That means our bodies are geared to work best when we follow that part of the owner's manual.

There are two options for applying the principle of extra Sabbath rest. The first is to sleep in on Sunday morning (but rising in time for church). The other is to maintain the habit of early rising you've already disciplined yourself to, and take a Sabbath rest on Sunday afternoon (after turning off the phone!).

Do whichever one works for you, but *do* follow God's ordained pattern. He knows best. Doing it God's way will also allow you to stay with it for the long haul, which leads me to our final chapter: How to make morning momentum a lifelong habit!

Chapter 11

Morning Momentum for a Lifetime

Often when I speak in a rural area, someone will approach me after the meeting and say, "I never have trouble getting up on time. I just wake up automatically without a clock." I then ask, "Were you raised on a farm?" 90% of the time they smile and say "Yes! We had to get up and milk the cows whether we felt like it or not!" Those "farmer's kids" were nursed with the secret sauce that enabled them with lifelong morning momentum- HABIT.

A habit is the behavior you do *by default*. You do it without even thinking about it or "deciding" to do it. The habits you form become a part of your nature. They define who you are and how you behave. They are powerful. That's why it is so important to understand a few concepts related to good morning habit formation.

Delayed Gratification

Every good habit stems from a thinking pattern which successful people are constantly developing. Brian Tracy, perhaps the foremost authority on peak performance, has done decades of research on the question of why some people achieve greatness while others flounder. He concludes that the ability to delay gratification is what makes the difference.[108]

Delayed gratification means putting off what I want *right now* to gain what I want *most*. It allows us to reject a second dessert to keep a healthy weight. It means getting a better education or learning a trade instead of grabbing for an immediate paycheck. It means young people directing their spending toward investments that produce a comfortable retirement instead of an overpriced daily treat at the coffee shop.[109]

I encourage you to make a lifelong quest after a daily routine that builds on delayed gratification. Begin each morning by denying yourself the instant gratification you crave at the moment (10 minute snooze), and replacing it with what you really want- time with God and being in control of your day. This topic is so fundamental to long term growth and success that I could easily write another book on it. But for now I'll encourage you to dig deeper by visiting LifeChangingSeminars.com and searching for delayed gratification.

Commitment

Another big difference between successful people and unsuccessful people, is that successful people do the things unsuccessful people don't like to do. They may not like to do them either, but that dislike is subordinate to the strength of their commitment and their determination to achieve God's best every day of their life.

Most people's goals program could be summarized as, "Set 'um and forget 'um." But without a commitment stronger than a garlic milkshake, you will likely never go from where you are now to a solid habit of morning momentum. Jesus pictured commitment as putting your hand to the plow and not looking back.[110] You can do this now by reviewing the accountability ideas from Chapter 2. Then, tell everyone you know about your new habit.

Staying Power

One reason old habits are so hard to break is that Satan doesn't easily yield his territory.[111] When we have allowed bad habits, such as morning slothfulness, to take hold, we have given him a "stronghold."[112] These are well entrenched territories that he won't give up without a fight. If you think otherwise, you are naive and the power behind your attempts at morning momentum will be fledgling, temporary and sporadic. Instead of the booming "dynamite" power

God offers to win the victory, it will more closely resemble the "snap crackle and pop" of Rice Krispies.[113]

I won't say that that making a lifetime habit of morning momentum *can't* happen if you don't recognize the spiritual component. But by doing so you leave out the greatest weapon at your disposal for effecting change. Jesus said, "Without me you can do nothing." But "With God, all things are possible."[114] That's a huge difference in results- nothing vs all things. It's like the power of a lightning bolt vs the power a lightning bug!

Ask God to give you the strength to keep steady at it when it's cold outside and you tell your legs to move, but they don't obey orders. Pray to Him and confess your weakness. Throw yourself at His mercy. He has promised to meet your need![115]

Repetition

An action becomes a habit by repetition. Early rising farm kids weren't "born that way." They acquired good habits through repetition. We only lose if we stop the repetition before the new habit takes hold. That's why many people despair over morning momentum. Zig Ziglar used to tell how some people were down on motivational speeches when they saw someone excited for a while after the event, but who later fell away. Zig pointed out that bathing was not permanent either. But he wasn't down on bathing simply because one application didn't do it for life!

View your new morning habits the same way. Put it on your calendar to reread this book in a few weeks. Your first reading will initiate vision, and hope for a positive change. A second or third reading will help solidify fledgling habits and produce even better results.

Do It NOW!

If you've made it this far in the book you are pretty determined to change. Now there is just one more obstacle we need to address. It is the one most likely to hinder you from launching.

Procrastination is the assassination of your motivation. When God gives a revelation of a new morning inclination, we get filled with inspiration, imagination, and anticipation. But then comes a hesitation, resulting in the evaporation of that determination and procrastination brings on the cancellation of your new morning stimulation. So don't procrastinate. Instead initiate!

"Tomorrow" is the Devil's favorite word. We can have good intentions but produce nothing unless we translate them into immediate action. You can have a heart of gold, but so does a boiled egg. What you need is a sense of urgency strong enough to make you take tangible steps to implement new morning habits right now. Some people dream of success, while others wake up early and make it happen.

Turning the Battleship

As you begin to implement change, it's vital to understand that God sometimes works in an instantaneous, breakthrough fashion to improve our morning habits. Picture a drill sergeant giving an "about face" command. But a more likely picture of how it actually happens would be a battleship captain ordering a U-turn. I prefer this illustration for two reasons.

First, when we expect total, immediate and complete change, we set ourselves up for discouragement at the first evidence of failure. While the change of direction must be *initiated* immediately, we may not complete the turn quite so fast. How we respond to those "failures" while we are still in the turnaround mode determines whether we will stay the course of change or remain adrift in currents of the status quo.

Morning momentum is not about perfection, but progress. Winston Churchill said, "Success is going from failure to failure without loss of enthusiasm." Solomon expressed the same thought this way, "A just man falls seven times and rises up again.[116]" A big wave may knock you temporarily off course while you are turning the ship around. But that's not sufficient grounds for abandoning the mission.

The second reason I prefer the battleship model, is the encouragement that comes from anticipating, and then experiencing, a *tipping point* somewhere in the middle of the turn, when the bow of the ship actually points in different direction.

It happens when you wake up one day just before your clock goes off. You realize something has changed. There is anticipation and excitement in the air. You are now getting up "on the right side of the bed" by default. You have already charted the course of an excellent day, beginning with the very first minute.

God is pleased with you. You have now mastered morning momentum and it feels wonderful!

[1] Hebrew 11:25-26

[2] Abraham, Genesis 9:27, Moses, Exodus 8:20, Gideon, Judges 7:1, Jesus, Mark 1:35

[3] Psalm 30:5

[4] Ephesians 5:14

[5] Revelation 22:16

[6] Isaiah 55:9

[7] Luke 24:1

[8] http://www.inspiringmoms.com/moms-stress-morning-stress-moms-family/

[9] Lamentations 3:22, 23a

[10] Proverbs 26:14

[11] Quote from Demetri Martin.

[12] If you want still more morning accountability, you can take a moment to ask one another accountability questions when you meet. The early Methodists held "Class Meetings," which were regular accountability sessions where the members asked probing questions to keep each other spiritually sharp. Learn more at http://www.goforthall.org/articles/jw_dscplshp.html

[13] Hebrews 10:24

[14] Hebrews 4:12

[15] Luke 9:62

[16] James 1:8

[17] Ecclesiastes 11:7

[18] Romans 13:14

[19] I am sometimes challenged on this point by those who think it would create extra laundry. But most of us don't throw a towel in the laundry after a single use. We wait until it is soiled. The two towel tactic means we use each towel only half as much, so we can use it twice as long, resulting in no added laundry.

[20] Proverbs 3:6

[21] There is even a waterproof songbook, "Hymns for the Shower" by Nat Wofford, available at Amazon.com.

[22] 8 Minutes in the morning, Jorge Cruise, Harper Collins, New York, 2002

[23] Romans 12:21

[24] Flight attendants always remind you to put on your own oxygen mask before helping your children with theirs. If you are overcome, you will be of no use to your children.

[25] Hebrews 10:24

[26] http://www.forbes.com/sites/jennifercohen/2013/10/02/5-things-super-successful-people-do-before-8-am/

[27] I am sometimes challenged about the environmental impact of paper plates. I remind skeptics that washing plates uses water and releases it into the environment with chemicals added. Hot water is normally produced by electricity which may have been generated at an environmentally unfriendly power plant. Paper comes from trees which are a renewable resource. I don't see much difference in impact. The math in this illustration also ignores the cost of washing dishes which includes water, water heating, electric for the dishwasher and the amortized cost of the dishwasher itself. Those likely equal the cost of the paper plates.

[28] Alan Lakein, *How to Get Control of Your Time and Your Life.* (New York: Wyden Publishers, 1973), 22.

[29] Isaiah 55:9.

[30] Job 1:3,5

[31] Job 7:18, 23:12b

[32] http://en.wikipedia.org/wiki/Stand-up_meeting

[33] James 3:5

[34] 1 Thessalonians 5:27

[35] Luke 9:16

[36] Proverbs 3:9

[37] Psalm 63:1, 2 Samuel 24:24

[38] Joshua 1:8

[39] http://livingbyfaithblog.com/2012/01/03/how-george-mueller-read-gods-word/#sthash.5JybS7wz.dpuf

[40] Mark 1:35

[41] Public Domain- Attributed to Grace L. Naessens

[42] http://www.gallup.com/poll/28504/workers-average-commute-roundtrip-minutes-typical-day.aspx Accessed 3/21/2012

[43] US Census Bureau- American Community Survey 2009.

[44] http://www.daveramsey.com/blog/20-things-the-rich-do-every-day

[45] 1 Peter 1:13

[46] John 6:12

[47] http://www.foxnews.com/story/0,2933,165217,00.html Accessed 3/27/12.

[48] http://www.nytimes.com/2007/12/09/magazine/09left-handturn.html Accessed 3/19/12.

[49] Romans 12:2

[50] Mark 12:39

[51] Isaiah 55: 8

[52] Colossians 3:9,10

[53] The Power of True Success- How to Build Character in Your Life" IBLP Oak, Brook IL 2001.

[54] Matthew 5:41

[55] http://www.fastcompany.com/3000619/what-successful-people-do-first-hour-their-work-day

[56] http://www.brainyquote.com/quotes/keywords/coffee.html>

[57] 1 Corinthians 6:12

[58] Keller, Gary, The ONE Thing, Bard Press, 2013. P. 201.

[59] Proverbs 3:6

[60] Be sure to check out this chapter's online resource for a list of creative responses to the question "How are you?" as well as other cheerful greetings.

[61] Leviticus 23:32

[62] 1 Timothy 2:9, Deuteronomy 22:5

[63] Matthew 6:30-31

[64] Steve Jobs, co-founder of Apple computer, determined early in his career to dress the exact same every day. He wanted to focus on building computers instead of deciding what to wear.

[65] Proverbs 20:11

[66] Proverbs 22:3

[67] http://www.mayoclinic.com/health/brushing-your-teeth/AN02098 Accessed 3/29/12.

[68] Ephesians 4:26, Matthew 5:24

[69] Deuteronomy 6:7

[70] Philippians 4:8

[71] Psalm 16:7

[72] Proverbs 13:20

[73] Job 1:5

[74] Judges 6:38

[75] Joshua 6:12, 8:10

[76] Genesis 22:3

[77] Exodus 8:20, 9:13

[78] 1 Samuel 9:26

[79] Daniel 6:18-19

[80] Psalm 63:1 Seeking God early can mean early in life, early when prompted to do so, or early in the morning.

[81] Mark 1:35 For more examples and encouragement on this topic, I recommend the booklet, "How to Conquer Slothfulness" from IBLP.org

[82] Mark 16:2 John 20:1

[83] http://www.rhema.org.sg/resources/175.html

[84] Strong's Concordance # 7836

[85] Proverbs 10:4

[86] Proverbs 31:15

[87] Proverbs 31:20,21

[88] http://www.daveramsey.com/blog/20-things-the-rich-do-every-day

[89] The first four items on the list come from research by RichHabitsInstitute.com cited on Ramsey's blog. The entire list is very insightful and well worth your time.

[90] http://www.forbes.com/pictures/lmj45hjhj/benefits-of-early-risers/

[91] Much of this list is gleaned from the article "29 Successful People Who Wake Up Really Early"
See the whole list at: http://www.businessinsider.com/successful-people-who-wake-up-really-early-2013-12?op=1#ixzz310cj5AO1

[92] Jonah 1:6

[93] Judges 16:19

[94] Matthew 26: 40-43

[95] Proverbs 12:24

[96] 1 Corinthians 9:25 NKJV

[97] http://www.webmd.com/sleep-disorders/news/20080609/early-birds-get-better-grades

[98] Ecclesiastes12.10

[99] Psalm 8:2 NKJV

[100] This short article gives a balanced perspective on this topic:
http://www.kindercare.com/blog/a-moms-point-of-view-the-bedtime-ritual/?utm_source=Outbrain&utm_medium=CPC&utm_campaign=Knowledge%20Universe%20-%20KinderCare%20Blog

[101] To find out more about this trip and how God worked it out for us to do on $10 per person per day, check out "The Mother of All Trips" at LifeChangingSeminars.com resource page.

[102] This also teaches a Biblical concept that if a person doesn't work, he should not be allowed to eat. 2 Thessalonians 3.10. Hunger is God's ordained cure for laziness.

[103] Galatians 5:13

[104] Psalm 119:147

[105] Treating serious depression is beyond the scope of this book. Don't be afraid to seek help from a professional, trained to give Biblical counsel. Just remember that there is a difference between getting Christian counseling and getting the counsel of the world from a Christian person.

[106] Titus 2:1-5

[107] Exodus 8:20, 9:13

[108] BrianTracy.com

[109] Proverbs 25:28 Tells of the spiritual danger of living for immediate gratification. It describes the life of such a person as a city vulnerable to enemy attack.

[110] Luke 9:62

[111] Ephesians 4:27

[112] 2 Corinthians 10:4

[113] God promises this power in Acts 1:8. The word He uses for "power" is the Greek word "dynamis". It is the same word from which we get the word "Dynamite".

[114] John 15:5, Mark 10:27

[115] In Philippians 4:13 Paul made an extraordinary claim that he could do "All things" through Christ and the strength He supplies.

[116] Proverbs 24:16